Wales
1880–1914

Edited by

Trevor Herbert
Gareth Elwyn Jones

Cardiff
University of Wales Press
1988

University of Wales Press, 6 Gwennyth Street, Cathays, Cardiff CF2 4YD

© The Open University, 1988

British Library Cataloguing in Publication Data

Wales 1880–1914 : Welsh history and its
  sources.
  1. Wales—History
  I. Herbert, Trevor   II. Jones, Gareth Elwyn
  942.9081   DA722

ISBN 0-7083-0967-4

Cover design : Cloud Nine Design

The publishers wish to acknowledge the advice and assistance given by the Design Department of the Welsh Books Council which is supported by the Welsh Arts Council.

Typeset by Megaron, Cardiff
Printed in Wales by Graham Harcourt (Printers) Ltd, Swansea

Welsh History and its Sources

Welsh History and its Sources is a project conducted at the Open University in Wales from 1985 to 1988 and funded by a Welsh Office Research Development grant. The project gratefully acknowledges the financial support made available by the Secretary of State for Wales.

Project Director:	Dr Trevor Herbert
Senior Visiting Fellow:	Dr Gareth Elwyn Jones
Steering Committee:	Mr O.E. Jones, H.M.I. (Chairman)
	Professor R.R. Davies, History Department, University College of Wales, Aberystwyth
	Mr N. Evans, Coleg Harlech
	Mr D. Maddox, Advisor, Mid Glamorgan LEA
	Mr A. Evans, Head of History Department, Y Pant Comprehensive School, Pontyclun
Secretary to the Project at the Open University in Wales:	Mrs Julia Williams

Contents

Illustrations

Maps and Diagrams

Contributors

DAVID EGAN is head of the history department in Mountain Ash Comprehensive School and tutor-counsellor for the arts foundation course at the Open University in Wales's Pontypridd study centre.

TREVOR HERBERT is sub-Dean, senior lecturer in Music and Arts Staff Tutor at the Open University in Wales. He specialises in British music history.

GARETH ELWYN JONES is Reader in history education in the department of education, University College of Swansea. He has taught various courses for the Open University in Wales and is currently an arts foundation course tutor-counsellor and assistant staff tutor.

KENNETH O. MORGAN is fellow and praelector in modern history at the Queen's College, Oxford. He is an international authority on Lloyd George. He has contributed to television programmes and has lectured at summer school for the Open University.

DAVID SMITH is professor in the history of Wales at University College, Cardiff. He is an accomplished radio and television broadcaster. He is a former tutor for the Open University in Wales.

L. J. WILLIAMS is senior lecturer in economics at University College, Aberystwyth.

TIMOTHY WILLIAMS studied history at Peterhouse, Cambridge. He now works for the National Union of Teachers.

Preface

This series gives an insight into Welsh history by examining its sources and the ways in which some leading historians use those sources. It is not formally a history of Wales. This volume, for instance, is not a chronological history of Wales in the period 1880–1914, neither is it a comprehensive history in the sense that its themes embrace all of the major issues and events that were important in the period. Readers of this book will, we hope, learn a great deal about Wales in the late nineteenth and early twentieth centuries but they will learn as much about the way in which professional historians interpret the raw materials of history. The choice of topics for the essays and documents collection was determined as much by the nature of the sources relevant to those topics as by the subject matter of the events or issues upon which they are based. Thus, John Williams's essay 'The Move from the Land' was chosen partly because it deals with matters critical to our understanding of the period, but also because the types of sources which he uses, mainly statistical, provide us with a sense of the value of those sources. Similarly, David Egan's essay 'Wales at Work' is based almost entirely on oral sources. The contributions of David Smith and Kenneth O. Morgan are examples of how, respectively, a particular significant episode and the life of one person of immense influence are tackled by the historian. Tim Williams treats a different area again in the complex theme of popular belief and culture, for which sources can be so emotive and nebulous.

At one level *Wales 1880–1914* is simply a book about the history of Wales at a time of rapid and epic change, and about the ways that historians interpret these changes. However, the series of which this volume is a part has been designed to serve a number of functions for anyone who is formally or informally engaged in a study of Welsh history. Those studying with a tutor, for instance extra-mural, university or sixth-form students, will find that it is a resource which will form a basis for, or enhance, a broader study of Welsh history. Those who are studying in a more remote location, far from formal classes in Welsh history, will find that the contents of the book are so ordered as to guide them through a course of study similar, but not analogous, to the methods which have proved successful in continuing education programmes of the Open University. The main feature of this method is that it attempts to combine a programmatic approach with something more flexible and open-ended.

Central to this book are Sections A to E which contain three different but closely-related and interlinked types of material. Each of these five essays is written on a clearly-defined topic. Each essay is immediately followed by a collection of source material which is the basis of the evidence for the essay. Within each essay reference is made to a particular source document by the inclusion of a reference number in the essay text; this reference number is also placed in the left-hand margin of the essay.

Each section also contains a discussion of the topic under the heading **Debating the Evidence**. The primary purpose here is to highlight the special features, weaknesses and strengths of each collection of sources and to question the way in which the author of the essay has used them. It is worth pointing out that we have not attempted here simply to act as *agents provocateurs*, setting up a series of artificial controversies which can be comfortably demolished. The purpose is to raise the sorts of questions which essayists themselves probably addressed before they employed these sources. In doing this we hope to expose the types of issues that the historian has to deal with. The discussion sections pose a number of questions about the sources. They do not provide model answers and neatly tie up all of the loose ends concerning each source. The discipline of history does not allow of that approach. If it did, there would be no need for a book of this type. The 'discussions' simply put forward a number of ideas which will cause readers to consider and reconsider the issues which have been raised. The purpose is to breed the kind of healthy scepticism about historical sources which underlies the method of approach of the professional historian.

Other parts of the book support these central sections. The Introduction poses basic problems about the difficulties of coping with historical sources, points which are consolidated in the Discussion sections. The intention of the opening essay, 'Wales 1880–1914', is to highlight immediately the problems of interpretation arising from the apparent discrepancy between a view of Wales outwardly prosperous and successful but at the same time wracked by industrial strife and dissension. At the end of the book is a glossary which briefly explains a number of the more technical terms and concepts arising out of the essays/documents collection. Although a glossary is properly a list of explanations of words and terms, we have, additionally, included brief details of persons who figure prominently in the essay and document material. Such words and names are *italicized* (thus).

Readers will, of course, decide how best to profit from the different constituent elements in the book. The first two chapters should certainly be read first, as these provide a context for the rest of the book. Some may then decide to read the five essays without reference to the source collections or discussion sections. This will form a broader framework for a re-examination of the essays with their sources and discussion sections.

The open-ended nature of the book serves to highlight the extent to which it has been our intention to do no more than *contribute* to an understanding of Welsh history. Different editors would have chosen different topics. The essays here should be seen within the framework of a much wider range of writings which, over the past few decades, has become available. The greatest success which a book like this can meet with is that it imparts to its readers an insatiable desire to know more about Welsh history and to do so from a standpoint which is constantly and intelligently questioning the ways in which historians provide that knowledge.

Acknowledgements

The development of the Welsh History and its Sources project was made possible by the support of the Secretary of State for Wales and I am happy to have made formal acknowledgement to the Secretary of State and individuals connected with the project elsewhere in this book.

Funding from the Open University made possible the development of the initial ideas that were eventually nurtured by a Welsh Office grant. The assistance of various individuals and departments of the Open University has been frequently and freely given. In particular, my colleagues at the Open University in Wales, where the project was based, have been constantly helpful. Julia Williams, secretary to the Arts Faculty of the Open University in Wales, acted as secretary to the project. As well as wordprocessing the texts for the entire series she was immensely efficient in the administration of the project. Picture copyright research was carried out by Rhodri Morgan. Editing for the University of Wales Press was done by Anne Howells and the Index compiled by Annette Musker.

University College of Swansea were kind enough to allow the part secondment of Dr Gareth Elwyn Jones to work on the project. Without him the project would not have progressed beyond being an idea as I have relied entirely on his widely respected expertise for overseeing the academic content of the series.

Two diverse contributions have enhanced the effectiveness of the material. Guy Lewis, University College of Swansea, drew the maps and diagrams, often from a jumble of data and instructions. Of crucial importance to the Discussion sections was the immensely helpful work of piloting the book with groups of students. This was undertaken by Neil Evans, colleagues and students at Coleg Harlech and by David Maddox, Christopher Despres, Raymond Bevan, Hefin Matthias,

Kenneth Morgan, John Wilson, colleagues and students from Mid Glamorgan County Council's Education Department.

My major debt of gratitude is to the contributors, each of whom was asked to write to a prescribed topic, format, word length and submission date. Each fulfilled his brief with absolute accuracy, punctuality and co-operation. The format was prescribed by me. Any shortcomings that this book may have can be put down to that prescription and to the consequences that emanated from it.

TREVOR HERBERT

Cardiff,
September 1986

Introduction

The essays contained in this book have been written not only by specialist historians, but also by specialists in the particular topic on which they have written. They are authorities on their subject and they make pertinent, informed and professional observations. Each essay is an important contribution to the historiography of Wales.

As specialists they know the sources for their topics intimately. They have included extracts from a cross-section of these sources to indicate on what evidence they base the generalizations and conclusions in their essays. We hope that the essays will interest you and that the documents will bring you into contact with kinds of primary sources which you may not have encountered before. Historians face a variety of problems when they consult source material and face even more difficulties when they have to synthesize the material collected into a coherent narrative and analysis of the events they are describing. In doing so the best historians make mistakes. Sometimes these are trivial (or not so trivial!) errors of fact. You may even spot factual discrepancies between information given in the various essays and the documents.

At the end of each essay/sources section there is a short discussion section. By the time you reach it you will have read the essay and the sources on which the essay is based.

The discussion section is concerned with problems of interpretation. It is an attempt to conduct a debate with the author about the way in which the essay relates to the sources. This is partly achieved by asking pertinent questions about the nature of the sources themselves. The intention is that you are stimulated to think about the validity of the exercise of writing history and the methodology of the study of history which is essentially what distinguishes it from other disciplines. The dialogue is a complex one and the questions posed do not, generally, have any 'right' answers. But they do have some answers which make more sense than others. We hope that the historians who have written the essays have provided answers which are reasonable. But historians are not infallible, however eminent they may be. Their conclusions are open to debate and discussion, as, for that matter, is their whole procedure of working. As you work through the discussion and questions you will notice that there is specific cross-referencing to the relevant section of the essay (or essays) and to documents. We hope this will be helpful since the success of the exercise depends vitally on taking into account the relationship between the primary source material and what the historian makes of it.

At the heart of the historian's task is the search for, and subsequent use of, evidence, much of it of the sort you will encounter here. The crucial distinction in the nature of this evidence is that between primary and secondary sources. There is no completely watertight definition of primary sources but a reasonable working definition would be that primary sources consist of material which came into existence during the period which the historian is researching, while secondary sources came into existence after that period. Whether or not a source can be regarded as primary or secondary relies as much on the topic of research as it does on the date of that source.

For example, consider the first of David Smith's sources (D.1), Churchill's election speech in Cardiff in 1950. It *seems* to be a primary source since Churchill was a central figure in events as they unfolded in Tonypandy in 1910. The example, in fact, is not as straightforward as it seems. This *is* a primary source for, say, the historian writing the history of Churchill's career. However, David Smith's topic is the Tonypandy riots of 1910. Churchill's speech was given decades after this event. Is it then a primary source for Professor Smith's topic? Why does the distinction matter?

Historical interpretation based on sources is extremely complex. It was once believed by highly reputable historians that if they mastered all the sources they could write 'true' history. There is at least one eminent historian who argues this now. You might like to consider on which side of the debate you stand at the moment.

Most historians would argue that this is impossible, that because we are removed from the time and place of the event that we are considering we are influenced by prejudices of nationality, religion or politics. However, there is some compensation for this because we know, usually, what the results were of actions which occurred during the period we are considering and this benefit of hindsight is enormously useful in trying to analyse the interplay of various factors in a situation and their influence on subsequent events. As you read the essays and documents in this collection, consider the degree of objectivity and subjectivity displayed by the authors. To do this you will need to consider what you would like to know about the authors before coming to a decision, and how far the authors are entitled to their own interpretations.

There is a similar pattern of work for each essay and its related documents. There are specific questions involving comprehension, evaluation, interpretation and synthesis, with synthesis, arguably, the highest level of the skills. However, there can be no rigid demarcation of historical skills such as interpretation and synthesis and some questions will overlap the various categories. There is no standard form of answer either as the discussions demonstrate. What the questions do provide is a structured pattern of work which will enhance understanding of the essays and documents.

Above all, there is dialogue and discussion about the way in which each historian has grappled with the complexities of writing about and interpreting the past. That such interpretation is as skilled, informed and mature as is conceivably possible is essential to our well-being as a society. In that these books are about the history of Wales they contribute fundamentally to the well-being of Welsh society. That well-being depends on debate, analytical, informed, structured debate. It is the purpose of this book to stimulate your involvement in that debate in a more structured way than has been attempted before in the study of the history of Wales.

Timechart

Wales		Other Significant Events
Liberals – 29 out of 33 seats. Welsh Rugby Union founded. Creation of National Eisteddfod Association.	**1880**	General Election – Gladstone Prime Minister.
Report of Aberdare Committee on Education. Welsh Sunday Closing Act.	**1881**	
	1884	Parliamentary Reform Act.
Liberals – 30 out of 34 seats. First Siemens open-hearth furnace at Brymbo.	**1885**	Redistribution Act – constituencies. General Election (November).
Liberals – 25 out of 36 seats. 1886/7 Creation of Liberal Federations of North and South Wales.	**1886**	Irish Home Rule Bill. General Election (July) – Marquess of Salisbury Prime Minister.
Formation of Ocean Coal Company.	**1887**	
	1888	Local Government Act creates County Councils.

Welsh Intermediate Education Act.	**1889**	
Barry Docks opened.		
Lloyd George becomes MP for Caernarfon Boroughs.	**1890**	
Tithe Rent Charge Act. O. M. Edwards founds *Cymru* (magazine).	**1891**	McKinley tariff on tinplate.
Liberals – 31 out of 34 seats.	**1892**	General Election (July) – Gladstone Prime Minister.
Cymru Fydd launched.		
Charter for University of Wales.	**1893**	
Royal Commission on Land. Explosion at Cilfynydd colliery killed 250.	**1894**	Tom Ellis becomes Liberal Chief Whip. Earl of Rosebery Prime Minister.
Liberals – 25 out of 34 seats.	**1895**	General Election (July) – Salisbury Prime Minister.
Effective end of *Cymru Fydd*. Report of Royal Commission on Land. Open hearth steelworks at Shotton. Creation of Central Welsh Board.	**1896**	
Six months stoppage in coal industry. Founding of South Wales Miners' Federation.	**1898**	
Death of Tom Ellis.	**1899**	Outbreak of Boer War.
Liberals – 28 out of 34 seats. Keir Hardie elected ILP MP for Merthyr. Penrhyn Quarry dispute starts.	**1900**	General Election (October) – Salisbury Prime Minister. Taff Vale railway dispute.

Welsh 'Revolt'.	**1902**	
Start of religious revival (Evan Roberts).	**1904**	
Wales defeat All Blacks in Cardiff. Cardiff achieves 'city' status.	**1905**	Lloyd George President of Board of Trade.
Liberals – 33 out of 34 seats.	**1906**	General Election – Campbell Bannerman Prime Minister.
Creation of Welsh Department of Board of Education.	**1907**	
	1908	Miners' Federation of Great Britain affiliates to Labour Party. H. H. Asquith becomes Prime Minister.
National Library of Wales founded. Plebs League founded.	**1909**	
Cambrian Colliery dispute. Tonypandy riots.	**1910**	Lloyd George's 'People's Budget' Campaign.
Investiture of Prince of Wales. Two railwaymen shot dead by troops in Llanelli.	**1911**	Lloyd George's National Health Insurance Act. National Railway Strike.
Establishment of Welsh Council of Agriculture. Welsh Commission for National Health Insurance Act. *Miners' Next Step* published.	**1912**	
Senghennydd colliery disaster, 439 killed.	**1913**	
Freddie Welsh lightweight champion of world. Welsh Church Act – Disestablishment.	**1914**	Outbreak of First World War (August).

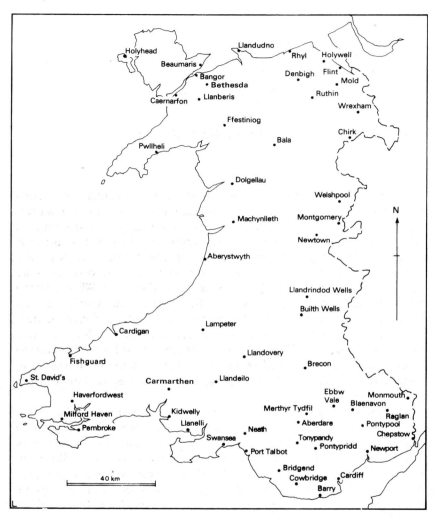

Place-name map of Wales.

Wales 1880–1914

GARETH ELWYN JONES

By the criteria conventionally used to measure the stature of nations Wales in the period 1880–1914 was a vibrant, proud, successful country. Industrial wealth had moved Wales from the margins of Britain to a position of world importance. Of the copper smelted in Britain in the nineteenth century 90 per cent came from south Wales, from Kidwelly in the west to Neath in the east. In 1898, the peak year for slate production, 70 per cent of UK slate was quarried in north Wales and the Penrhyn and Dinorwic quarries were the biggest in the world. In 1902 the biggest nickel works in the world were built in Clydach, near Swansea, by *Sir Alfred Mond*. Between 1914 and 1918 the Swansea area produced 75 per cent of Britain's zinc. The tinplate industry was created in west Wales and just before the First World War 82 works from Llanelli to Port Talbot were producing 823,000 tons of tinplate, 544,000 tons of which were for export.

The most dramatic expansion had occurred in the coal industry. In 1911, 14,500 men were employed in the north Wales coal industry in Denbighshire and Flintshire, but it was in south Wales that growth took place on an unprecedented scale. In 1913 there were 485 collieries in Wales, 323 in Glamorgan. In 1885 the Rhondda pits produced 5,500,000 tons of coal, by 1913 this had risen to 9,500,000 tons. Forty-one thousand miners were employed in Rhondda pits alone. South Wales was producing about one third of world coal exports. In 1901, 46 per cent of Britain's coal exports went from south Wales to Europe, South America and the Middle East. In the process the great coal-exporting ports of Cardiff, Swansea, Barry and Newport had mushroomed.

Economic growth was matched by population growth in industrial Wales. In the second half of the nineteenth century people were flooding into the south Wales coalfield at a rate only exceeded in the United

States. The population of the Rhondda valleys in 1861 was 12,000; in 1891, 128,000. This meant that Rhondda's population was far higher than that of any Welsh county in 1801. Glamorgan's population of nearly one and a quarter million in 1911 was more than that of the whole of Wales in 1851. There were now very large thriving conurbations in Wales. Cardiff's population exceeded 100,000 and Swansea's was not too far behind, reflecting the prosperity of the commercial and business infrastructure of this society.

Politically, Wales appeared both to be united and to reflect the self-confidence resulting from such a prosperous economic base. The politics of deference had not ended in 1868 but the *Ballot Act* of 1872, the achievement of household suffrage in 1884 which had enfranchised significant numbers of the working class, and the *Local Government Act* of 1888 gave Liberals control of both national and local government. With the inauguration of urban and district councils in 1894 the domination of the landed gentry, exercised since Tudor times, over the government of Wales, was finally broken. The alliance between Liberalism and nonconformity was virtually complete during the period. The leadership of a largely professional and commercial middle class, farmers, shopkeepers, ministers, solicitors, was accepted, with endorsement from the working class. In the election of 1880, 29 out of 33 Welsh parliamentary seats were won by Liberals; in 1885, 30 out of 35. From 1892 to 1895 Welsh Liberal MPs actually held the balance of power and were particularly effective in highlighting Welsh concerns. In 1906 only one Welsh seat was not won by a Liberal, and that was *Keir Hardie*'s Labour seat in Merthyr.

There were Liberal achievements both within and without the party. In the 1880s the internal organization of the party was tightened up, with two Liberal *Federations* formed, one for north Wales and one for south, although there was a crisis in 1894–5.

From the 1880s the dynamic leadership of *Tom Ellis* and Lloyd George had produced a less quiescent brand of Liberalism and they both endorsed the *Cymru Fydd* movement for Welsh home rule. Originally this policy had also been supported by coalowner *D. A. Thomas*, but he soon turned to opposition, reflecting the views of the south Wales commercial community whose priorities were far removed from notions of Welsh independence. The crisis was short-lived. Within two years Lloyd George was again co-operating with the south Wales Liberals and the separatist movement in Wales was, in any case, never very strong.

This episode really serves to highlight the considerable achievements of a more restrained nationalism which was the hallmark of Welsh Liberalism – a striving for national respectability, for parity with England, for recognition of national differences. Here the achievements of Liberalism were impressive, although of course dependent on the Liberal Party being in government. In the 1880s Welsh – and English – Liberals forged Welsh demands for educational reform, land reform, *disestablishment* of the Church of England in Wales and some measure of devolution into a programme of concern to Liberalism nationally. In 1881 came the Aberdare report on education which resulted in the *Welsh Intermediate Education Act* of 1889, the establishment of a network of secondary schools over Wales subsidised by the Treasury – a remarkable achievement. The Welsh university colleges were also to receive grants and the University of Wales received its charter in 1893.

From 1886 the Welsh land question was at the forefront of attention, accentuated by agricultural depression. The *betes-noires* of Welsh society were the landed gentry, English-speaking, Anglican, absentee, rich, having acquired their riches by the exploitation of a Welsh-speaking, Nonconformist tenantry who had been victimized in a variety of ways. This victimization took the form of non-compensation for improvement to holdings, and, above all, eviction for political principle when they had refused to vote for their landlord's nominee at elections. The evictions of the 1860s were real enough, if exaggerated. Some of the other indictments had far less substance. But the myths, carefully fostered, could be more potent than reality and there was nothing imaginary about the agricultural depression. In 1891 the *Tithe Rent Charge Act* made *tithe* payable by the landowner, though of course this did not satisfy Liberal opinion. In 1893 came a royal commission into the land question, though by the time its two conflicting reports emerged a *Tory* government was in power and no action followed. In any case a changed situation by the time the Liberals were next in power in 1906 made the question less urgent.

The issue of the payment of *tithes* was satisfactorily, even triumphantly, solved with eventual *disestablishment*. The iniquities of a predominantly Nonconformist nation being subjected to the payment of *tithes* to the Anglican church had long stirred Welsh Liberals. Natural justice was flouted by the refusal of Anglicans to bury Nonconformists in consecrated ground. There was the constant problem of Anglican schools, since there were over 300 school districts in Wales where the only available elementary education was in a Church school. Liberal strength in Wales enabled Lloyd George to lead a revolt against the implementation of the 1902 *Education Act*. In north Wales 175 out of 260 councillors were Liberals, in south Wales 215 out of 330. Breconshire was the only county controlled by the *Tories*. Not surprisingly Lloyd George was able to unify the Liberal party nationally and locally in opposition to rate aid being given to the voluntary schools. A policy of non-co-operation with the government followed and the conflict was not resolved until the Liberals were once more in power in 1906. Here was a significant national revolt against the traditional enemy.

The pinnacle of Liberal achievement was the eventual granting of *disestablishment* in 1914, to be implemented after the war. Other monuments to Welsh cultural nationalism and distinctive legislative treatment are not hard to find. When the Liberals were in government from 1906 Wales was granted a *Welsh Department of the Board of Education*, a National Library, a National Museum, a Welsh Insurance Commission and a National Council for Wales for Agriculture.

Respectable Victorian opinion valued religious observance highly and, according to the criteria of chapel accommodation and attendance, the Welsh were a very religious people. Temperance movements, *Bands of Hope*, emotional preaching, the Sunday School, chapel societies, chapel choirs, *cymanfaoedd canu*, were woven into the fabric of Welsh society, rural and industrial. Wales had produced more than its share of outstanding pulpit orators, *Christmas Evans, John Elias, Herber Evans, Elfed Lewis*. Their effect was dramatic: 'wave after wave of emotion would pass over and thrill through the vast congregation, until it was seen to move and sway to and fro as the trees of the wood are moved by the wind'. Occasionally the waves of emotion would spread through the nation. Revivals tended to be localized, but there had been national revivals in 1840 and 1859. There was another, more unconventional, in 1904, fostered by the intense, emotional fervour of *Evan Roberts*. There were Bible studies, prayer meetings, and, above all, preaching. For three years his hold was remarkable, though the Nonconformist establishment, now highly respectable, was rather alarmed. Perhaps it is not surprising that new, dislocated communities, growing at such a rate at the turn of the century, flooded with people whose roots were often in rural Wales, should respond to an appeal which offered old values in a new environment. For a few years the revival was certainly effective. The chapels claimed that their membership increased by 90,000. In

4

Wales in 1906 total membership stood at 549,000 – and that ignores adherents.

For a short time it seemed that *Evan Roberts*'s revival would nip in the bud the remarkable growth in south Wales of a public school game which had been embraced by all classes in Wales. Rugby football clubs closed as members were convinced of the inherent sinfulness of that, or any other, game, but not for long. For even in the sport of the English, Irish and Scottish upper-middle class the Welsh were proving particularly adept, whether in tactical innovation or in winning games. The event which caught the public imagination and entered Welsh folk-lore was the defeat of the seemingly invincible *New Zealand All Blacks* in 1905.

Economic growth, political achievement, educational progress, religious fervour and sporting prowess seem to be the hallmarks of Welsh life in this period – and would be difficult to parallel elsewhere in the nation's history. They contrast dramatically with what was to follow in the 1920s and 1930s. Historians would agree that the factual basis of this analysis is reasonable and accurate. The facts themselves can be checked against a variety of sources – census returns, government statistics and reports, newspaper accounts, *Hansard*. Historians would agree also that the analysis so far has been highly selective, that it concentrates on the positive and emphasizes the achievement and the consensus. They would want to redress the balance by showing another Wales.

There were influential Welshmen in the period whose view of their country had a considerable impact. *Sir O. M. Edwards* (d. 1920), historian and litterateur, produced two extremely important magazines, *Cymru* and *Cymru'r Plant*. These, his book on the history of Wales and his many other writings, evoked a Wales which was in essence an idyllic rural country, with a people who had struggled valiantly against oppression through the centuries, and retained the virtues of a generally classless people, Welsh-speaking, skilled at rural crafts, law-abiding. For such a people struggles against the oppression of landlords and alien Church were in the mainstream of history. The increasing emphasis of *Edwards* and other scholars on the rural, peasant existence was romanticized and distorted the whole nature of nineteenth-century Welsh history, with its rapid industrialization. But even for those to whom the essence of Welshness lay in the mountains of Snowdonia and the tenant farms of Bala the situation in the late nineteenth century was extremely worrying.

As we have seen, the second half of the nineteenth century had witnessed a revolutionary demographic change. At the beginning of the century the population was roughly evenly divided between north and south. By 1900 Glamorgan and Monmouthshire were overwhelmingly preponderant. Rural Wales was not only losing its natural increase in population, numbers were actually declining. Anglesey's population went down from 57,000 to 50,000 between 1851 and 1911. The movement from the land into industrial Wales gathered momentum in the 1880s and 1890s with agricultural depression, although it did slow down after 1900. Was it the case, then, that the values and language of rural Wales were being transported to industrial areas as had happened to a considerable extent in the early nineteenth-century? Far less so in the late nineteenth century because mixed in with Welsh migration was an increasing element of English immigrants. In 1871 9.6 per cent of the population of south Wales came from English counties. By 1891 the proportion was 16.5 per cent. Each decennial census revealed that the number of Welsh speakers, proportionately not absolutely, was declining.

The move from the land into industrial Wales accentuated the disparity between the two parts of the country – in population, in resources and in life-style. The great Liberal leaders of the late nineteenth century, *Tom Ellis* and Lloyd George, were products of the rural north. *Cymru Fydd* foundered because commercial interests in the south would accept nothing other than the predominant influence in Wales. Central Liberal policies – land reform, *disestablishment* – were less relevant to industrial Wales. Liberalism never really developed incisive social policies to answer the needs of industrial communities. The world of official Liberalism seemed far removed from that of labour unrest, riots, lock-outs, class conflict, confrontation.

Coal brought wealth to south Wales but that wealth was not evenly distributed. Successive *marquesses of Bute, dukes of Beaufort*, and *Morgans of Tredegar* made 3d to 10d per ton of coal in royalties without actually having to be involved in the production process at all. For the owners in the great coal combines, Ocean or Powell Dyffryn, there were fortunes to be made. For the men who dug the coal there were fluctuating wages according to a *sliding scale*, the ever present danger of roof falls and gas explosions or the steady invasion of lung-tissue by coal dust. Between 1851 and 1855, 738 men and boys died in pit accidents in south Wales and Monmouthshire. After legislation and inspection there was an improvement but families and communities were faced with the constant threat of tragedy. In 1913 it came to Senghennydd. An explosion killed 439 men. Colliers were convinced that out of the enormous wealth which accrued to the coalowners they spent wholly inadequate sums on safeguarding the lives of the men who dug the coal.

Consensus could not survive disputes over wages when coalowners took an intransigent attitude, as they did. In 1898 miners wanted a 10 per cent increase on the rate used for calculating the *sliding scale*. There was a six-month stoppage, the owners yielded not an inch, the miners were defeated and in the aftermath the *South Wales Miners' Federation* was born. In 1910–11 there was a one-year stoppage in the Cambrian combine. In October 1910, 12,000 men had stopped work and in the following month they were joined by Rhondda miners. *Blacklegs* were brought in to break the strike, there was violence as police and rioters clashed and one miner died from a fractured skull. The coalowners refused any compromise, *Winston Churchill* authorized the sending of troops. This was confrontation, not consensus. In the year when the miners of Aberdare and the Rhondda valleys were defeated there was a national railway strike. In August, 1911, troops shot and killed two railway workers in Llanelli.

In north Wales there had already been confrontation which blended old causes and new, a struggle between Nonconformist, Welsh-speaking workmen and landowning capitalists. It had taken place in the slate industry. *Lord Penrhyn*, owner of one of the largest slate quarries in the world was also owner of the third largest estate in Wales. In 1896–7 there was a confrontation in which the men were defeated after eleven months. In 1900 another dispute led to the 2,800-strong labour force being locked out. *Lord Penrhyn*, with his vast resources of wealth, could afford to forgo his slate profits, aware that this fight was for the preservation of a social and economic power structure in which men like himself were utterly dominant. The quarrymen had no resources once meagre union funds ran out. They were helped by the British trade union movement, but such aid could only be minimal. Some men and their families came close to starvation, many emigrated, many moved south. The men lost, as did the slate industry. In the end the vast estates of men like *Penrhyn* were to go, too.

Confrontation in labour relations was paralleled by the growth of a new politics. Of course the Liberal hold on Wales, at Westminster and in local government, remained firm in this period but after the 1898 dispute in the coal industry *Independent Labour Party* branches spread in industrial Wales, in Merthyr, Swansea and Wrexham. In 1900 *Keir Hardie* was elected ILP member for Merthyr. By 1900 there were Labour councillors in Swansea and by 1905 there were 27 ILP branches in Wales. In 1908 the *Miners' Federation of Great Britain* affiliated to the Labour Party and miners' MPs joined the Labour Party in the Commons.

In 1909 *Noah Ablett*, a marxist advocate of the overthrow of capitalism and its replacement by workers' control, was instrumental in founding the *Plebs' League* in Rhondda. In 1912, from an unofficial reform committee of the *South Wales Miners' Federation*, came *The Miners' Next Step*, a remarkable and influential document which advocated a 7-hour working day, an 8*s* per day minimum wage and most significant, workers' control of the coalmines to be achieved by strikes and industrial action. Here indeed was an alternative politics.

Virtually all aspects of Welsh life in this late-Victorian, Edwardian period, seemingly vital, prosperous, politically successful, can be viewed from another direction. To take only one more example, the *Welsh Intermediate Education Act of 1889* had resulted in county schools being set up in every Welsh county by 1896. This was a fine achievement, representing a commitment to exemplary community values and to the future. Yet in the years before the First World War the schools, and the *Central Welsh Board* which examined and inspected them, were being increasingly criticized for providing the kind of education which was betraying the linguistic, cultural and social needs of Wales.

It is perhaps more general for historians to catalogue the very real achievements of the period in Wales. Yet none would deny the paradoxes and the tensions they concealed. The historians who write the essays which follow have explored some of the questions which emerge from these paradoxes. They have not written conventional textbook accounts of their theme, to add to received 'truth' about the period, the books and the articles in historical journals. But in the last resort historical paradoxes, contradictions and tensions can only be explored and illuminated by resort to the documents and other types of source – the raw material with which the historian works according to strictly defined principles.

Exploration of the sources will not provide definitive answers, but it will produce new information, new questions, new perspectives.

As we have seen, the historian of Wales in this period has plenty of problems to explore and some of them are treated in the ensuing essays. The object of the essays is to show historians at work on important themes from the perspective of some of the essential primary sources for that time. They will make statements, come to some conclusions, but, more important, relate their judgements to specific primary sources, so demonstrating why some are tentative, others more firmly based, why there are some questions which cannot be answered. The material rests on a wide range of primary sources. Historians ask similar questions of them all. Why did the source come into existence? Who was its author? Was its author in a good position to know about the event recorded? What bias – political, personal, social – was the author likely to display, and is there evidence in the source for it? What actual historical information does the source provide intentionally? Often more important, what information not intentionally conveyed by the author, does the source yield about the period and, indeed, about its author?

Such questions are always at the back of historians' minds. In answering them they establish the reliability of their evidence which, of course, materially affects their conclusions. They know well that some sources are more reliable than others. Census returns for this period are accurate and informative – we know the processes by which the material was collected and collated. A private letter from a politician may reveal more about his attitude to a particular policy than a speech in the House of Commons, though the motives for both may not be as they seem. Newspaper accounts are the only source for many events, yet they have to be treated with great circumspection. What is the editor's political stance – or that of the proprietor? 'Factual' reports are often of dubious accuracy.

Photographs are an invaluable source for architecture, dress and leisure activities, for example, but the camera can misinform just like written sources. With the period ending in 1914 historians are just able to make use of oral testimony. The reminiscences of people living in the period with which historians are concerned are unique and can be invaluable, but again have to be treated with great caution and checked as rigorously as possible with other information. Memories are faulty and selective. Experience and hearsay easily mingle. Implicitly and explicitly historians are constantly analysing the reliability of their sources. They are also constantly asking questions of them. For example, census returns yield a mass of information but the raw data have to be interpreted. In the hands of the specialist historian

9

information about population density, migration or linguistic patterns, for example, will be built up to illumine judgements about the state of a nation. The essays and their accompanying documents show historians at work on different types of sources central to the period. As well as augmenting our knowledge of the period the essays illuminate the historian's craft.

The Move from the Land

JOHN WILLIAMS

There are many rewards for attempting to understand the past, but success is not likely to be one of them. This is because the factors which shape the development of economies, societies and nations are infinite, and infinitely varying. Societies may be manipulated (to a degree) by personalities or parties; they may be influenced by more or less identifiable dramatic events; they may be constrained by established institutions and customs; and they may be affected by broad, anonymous movements. Population changes mostly fall within the last category. They steal silently on but may be more continuously significant than such more obtrusive considerations as strikes, riots, Lloyd Georges, Liberal parties and Nonconformist chapels.

At the very least, it is perfectly obvious that all aspects of modern history have been crucially influenced by the unprecedented acceleration in population growth. In the nineteenth century this affected, especially, Europe; in the twentieth century, the world as a whole. One immediate accompanying feature has been the shifts in population as people moved both within nations and between nations. Wales was by no means immune from these broad trends. In 1801 the population of Wales was 587,245; in 1851, 1,163,000; in 1901, 2,013,000. The nineteenth-century pattern, therefore, was for population to double in the first half century, and then to (almost) double again in the second half: this roughly reflected the pattern for Great Britain as a whole. For Wales, the most dramatic increase came at the end of our period. In the single decade from 1901 to 1911 the population of Wales increased by over 400,000 people. Wales thus, at least fully shared in the general nineteenth-

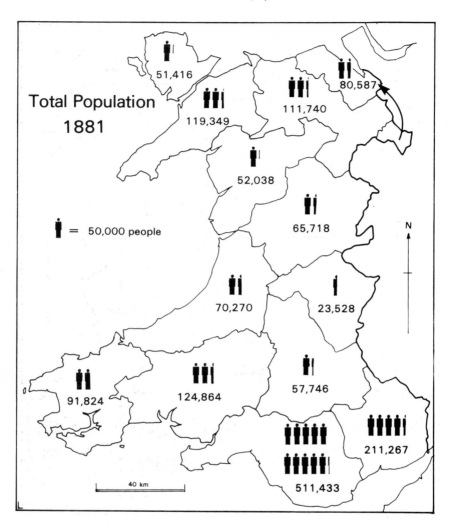

Total Population
1881

= 50,000 people

51,416

119,349

111,740

80,587

52,038

65,718

70,270

23,528

91,824

124,864

57,746

211,267

511,433

N

40 km

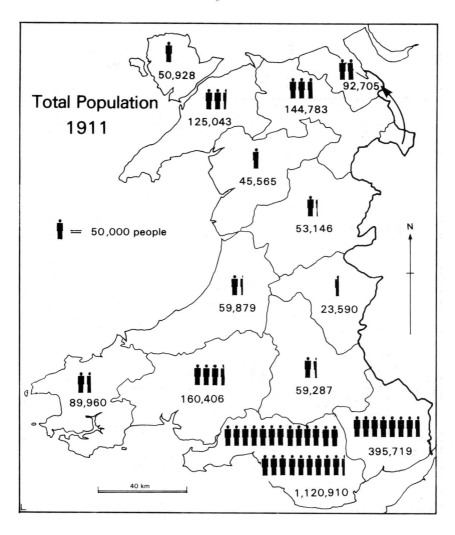

Total Population
1911

50,928

125,043

144,783

92,705

45,565

53,146

= 50,000 people

59,879

23,590

N

89,960

160,406

59,287

395,719

1,120,910

40 km

century population explosion. It also experienced the general tendency for population to be redistributed: in the case of Wales this took the form of the balance of the population slipping towards the bottom – in 1801 less than 20 per cent of the population of Wales was in the two counties of Glamorgan and Monmouthshire; by 1911 almost 63 per cent of the people were in these two counties. (Throughout this essay, the old 13 counties of Wales will be used, since this is the form in which all the census material exists.) Only one part of this story will be taken up here. However, that part – the move from the land – was particularly characteristic of the period from 1880 to 1914.

How do we know this? It is not as straightforward as it might seem to identify the Welsh rural exodus. The movement does not show up in vast decreases of population in the agricultural areas. Indeed, in only two counties (Cardigan and Montgomery) was the population in 1911 significantly below that of 1851. There are, moreover, no direct figures on migration in the census returns for this period. Such considerations should make us view statements about migration with care, if not scepticism. None the less, the broad picture can be inferred with reasonable confidence from at least two considerations. In the first place we know from the general census figures that the population of England and Wales, and the population of Wales itself, almost exactly doubled between 1851 and 1911. We also know that the increase must have arisen because more people were born and/or fewer died and/or there was a net movement of people into these countries: but we do not know with any certainty why birth and death rates change or even why people migrate. In other words, the immediate causes of population change are relatively few and simple (births: deaths: migration) but the ultimate causes are numerous and elusive. Fortunately for the present purpose certainty over final causes is not necessary. It is enough to notice that the differences in the rates of population change between the different Welsh counties are too great to make it likely that they could be explained simply and wholly by different birth and death rates. Which means that migration must have played a part. Indeed, some of the variation in birth and death rates was itself the result of migration. The movement of people into some areas and out of others would, of course, influence the age structure of the population of particular areas and this *would*, over time, influence the crude birth and death rates (i.e. the rate expressed per 1,000 of total population regardless of the age structure). Even apart from this, however, differences between the rates of population increase in different counties are likely to be mainly due to migration.

This inference is strengthened by the second consideration. It is possible to calculate the amount and rate of natural increase (i.e. the excess of births over deaths) for each county from 1841 onwards. For every county in Wales for every decade up to 1911 this figure was positive. The population of each county should thus have risen by the amount of the natural increase: in many cases, however, the actual increase was much less (and in some counties for some decades even showed an actual decline). The difference can only be due to people having moved out of those particular counties.

A.1   The pattern of net migration which emerges for the Welsh counties from this exercise is quite complex (A.1). None the less a few basic points relevant to our problem stand out quite starkly. In particular, starting with the decade ending in 1851, there are five Welsh counties – Brecon, Cardigan, Montgomery, Pembroke and Radnor – which experienced a *net loss* by A.2   migration in every single decade (A.2). Moreover, in four other counties – Anglesey, Carmarthen, Flint and Merioneth – there was a *net loss* in every decade except one.

These counties then constitute the main losers by migration in the half-century or so before 1914. Before we can conclude that this represented a move from the land, however, we need to know what was happening to the total population of these counties during these decades, and to have some reasonable indicator that the movement represented a shift away from agriculture. The need for caution on the first point can be illustrated from the experience of Carmarthen. As already indicated, this county suffered a net loss through migration in every decade except that of 1901–11. None the less, in every single decade there was an increase in the total population. In other words the net migration was only removing part of the natural increase in population. There was movement away but

Binding corn into sheaves, Brechfa, Dyfed, *c.*1898. (*Source: Welsh Folk Museum.*)

there were always more people left. Whether this constituted a movement from the land is a nice question.

Of course it is possible, even likely, that in Carmarthenshire there was an actual decrease in the agricultural population which was being more than offset by increases in the industrial sectors of the county. Clearly a much more detailed study would be required before such a pattern could be established with certainty: the need for caution is indicated by the broad fact that the number of males in agriculture only fell from 12,900 to 11,300 between 1851 and 1911 (G. B. Longstaff, 'Rural Depopulation', *Journal of the Royal Statistical Society*, LVI, 1893, Tables IV and V illustrate this). The same could be said of other counties in which there were usually net losses by migration but persistent gains in total population. These counties were Caernarfon, Denbigh and Monmouth. Glamorgan was the only county to make a net gain from migration in every decade, and of course it made large gains in total population in each decade. Monmouthshire is particularly interesting since, despite heavy industrialization, it experienced a net loss by migration in four of the seven decades after 1851 although the size of the natural increase (excess of birth over deaths) ensured that the total population rose in each decade. Indeed, the county is in some respects too large a unit to capture the 'move from the land'. All counties, however seemingly rural, have urban centres and pockets of industry or mining. Some of the complications of this have just been indicated (an attempt to define the rural population more precisely is given in A. L. Bowley, 'Rural Population in England and Wales', *Jnl. Roy. Stats. Soc.*, LXXVII, 1914). But in other important respects, the crudity of the county as a unit is an advantage. The essence of the 'move from the land' as an issue in Welsh historical experience is not a concern about shifts within a county but about a fundamental change in the balance of the population between different regions of the county as a whole.

At all events, the real hall-mark of the counties where out-migration was the most characteristic demographic feature was: a persistent *net loss* of population by migration accompanied by frequent decades in which there was also an absolute decline in the total population. The counties so affected were Brecon, Cardigan, Merioneth (for our particular period from 1800 onwards), Montgomery and Radnor. These were the counties which experienced an unequivocal outwards movement. Was it also a movement from the land?

The most useful indicator of that would be to see if these counties were primarily agricultural. And *that* can be best shown by looking at the proportion of the total working population engaged in agriculture (A.3). On this basis it turns out that the counties where out-migration was most marked were those which were most heavily agricultural. Even in 1911, when for Wales as a whole less than 12 per cent of occupied Wales worked on the land, Radnor, Montgomery and Cardigan each had around one-half of their male workers in agriculture (Merioneth had one-third, and Brecon nearly one-quarter).

What has been stressed so far is that population movements are complicated and often confusing, especially in the absence of any direct census information on migration. None the less it has been more or less conclusively inferred from the evidence that there was a substantial redistribution of the population within

A.3

Wales and that one significant feature of these shifts was a movement of people away from the countryside. It is still not possible to identify with any certainty just who moved, but there are strong indications that one element was an outflow from agriculture itself. In the first place, the total number engaged in agriculture in Wales, despite a doubling of the total population, actually declined between 1851 and 1911 (most of the decline being in the number of farm workers and not in the number of farmers). Even more suggestive is the fact that the rate of decline was generally most steep in the more agricultural counties (A.4). In five counties (Brecon, Cardigan, Merioneth, Monmouth and Montgomery), the number of males occupied in agriculture in 1911 was less than three-fifths of the number for 1851. Four of these counties were heavily agricultural, the oddity again being Monmouthshire. An important group contributing to the out-migration was clearly made up of those who had been, or would have been, occupied in agriculture.

A.4

The question of who moved raises another, and perhaps more interesting, issue. There is a strong general presumption that the rural counties lost the most able, energetic and industrious section of their population. But did they? The question is fundamentally intractable. The assumption that the best would move is plausibly based on the proposition that only the most able would both see, and seek out, the opportunities opening out in other regions (A.5). Still, the draining-away of those of the highest quality ought not simply to be presumed. It is also plausible, perhaps equally plausible, to argue that in a declining, highly competitive agricultural environment only the best would come to own farms and make them pay: the rest would have been driven out. It is often those who have been least successful in a given environment who are squeezed out and this should at least call into question the presumption that the agricultural areas are necessarily losing their most able people. What is true, of course, is that the migrants tended to be concentrated in the younger age groups. Indeed, this is in itself one reason for the general assumption that the agricultural areas lost their most able people: in the context of the nineteenth century it was quite reasonable to confuse strongest with best.

A.5

The question of who moved is closely connected to that of

why they went. At one level each individual has his own unique set of motives; at another level these can be reduced to a limited number of generalisations. Indeed, some would argue that all the motivations for migrating can be reduced to just two categories: carrots and sticks. All those factors which positively attract the migrant towards somewhere new are categorized as carrots: all those factors which are looked upon as driving people away from a particular area are categorized as sticks. But they are often simply the same phenomenon looked at from a different stand-point. Thus there is ample testimony that agricultural wages in nineteenth-century Wales were relatively low (the stick), and equally that the expectation of higher wages

A.6   in industrial areas acted as a magnet (the carrot) (A.6). These wage differentials were a permanent feature, but they were reinforced when, in the late nineteenth century, agriculture was generally depressed and declining because of intensified competition from overseas whilst industrial south Wales was still exhibiting strong long-term growth. Ultimately, however, these are just illustrations of the simple over-riding fact. People moved because there was not enough work for them in the

A.7   countryside (A.7). The decline in the numbers employed in agriculture was the most visible and symbolic aspect of this, but there was a general tendency for many economic activities to

A.8   move away from rural communities (A.8, A.9).

A.9   Another aspect of this which on the face of it seems a likely cause of movement was that technical change in agriculture was reducing the need for labour. This is given additional plausibility by the fact that the movement out of agriculture was mostly a reduction in the number of agricultural labourers and not in the number of farmers. None the less, the use of

A.10   machinery seems to have played little part in this process (A.10). Most of the reduction took place because one of the effects of foreign competition was to drive Welsh agriculture towards heavier concentration on *pastoral* as against *arable farming*: between 1867 and 1914 the total acreage under permanent pasture in Wales increased from 1,500,000 to 2,300,000, whilst that under *arable* cultivation fell from 1,100,000 to 700,000 acres.[1] One consequence of this was a reduction in the demand for agricultural labourers because in general *pastoral farming* is less labour-intensive.

What does not appear to have happened is that the movement from the land meant an abandonment of the land. Indeed, the report on Welsh agriculture produced for the Royal Commission on Labour spoke confidently of a land hunger shown in strong competition for farms as they became vacant. The problem was rather that with competition increasing (natural increase – the excess of births over deaths – remained positive) many felt that their aspirations for a farm of their own were unlikely to be fulfilled. Opportunities thus seemed to be closing in many rural areas making the possibilities elsewhere seem more attractive. All this was, moreover, not simply a matter of economic considerations. What were perceived by some as the constraints of rural life could help to persuade people to move, whilst others saw these same features as bestowing a cosy community which would help to tie them to an area. Similarly, some saw in the towns only delights, others mainly perceived

A.11 dangers (A.11). Such intangibles certainly exerted a strong influence, though whether it was to pull or to push depended on individual perceptions. And perhaps it was possible to get, or attempt to get, the best of both worlds. Thus a recent detailed study of Merthyr in 1851 reveals a strong tendency for immigrants from different parts of Wales to live in their own distinct areas within the town.[2] If people were, for whatever reason, moving from the land, to where were they going? A generation ago the impression left by the histories of this period was that the exodus from rural Wales typically ended in

A.12 settlement outside Wales altogether (A.12). It was an inference which was natural enough. The stream of overseas settlers was the most conspicuous group. Their departures, having an air of finality, made more impact, their letters home were more likely to be printed in the local press. And it was a movement punctuated by dramatic moments – the consciously communal move to *Patagonia* in the 1860s, or to *Philadelphia* in the 1890s (though the latter was less a flight from the – agricultural – land than a response by the Llanelli tin-plate workers to the *McKinley tariff*). Even the less romantic flow to England created communities in several of the main English towns which were

A.13 conspicuously Welsh (A.13). The picture of a movement which was typically away from Wales altogether is one which has more recently been substantially demolished by much careful statistical work, especially by Brinley Thomas.[3]

The picture which now emerges is more complex but the broad outlines can be briefly indicated. It is true that for Wales as a whole there was normally a *net loss* by migration. But this was the case for all the constituent countries of the United Kingdom and the loss, as a proportion of the total population, was much greater for Scotland, very much greater for Ireland and (from 1880 on) greater even for England. Still more striking is the fact that the only decade in which any of these countries registered a net gain through migration was for Wales from 1901 to 1911 (A.14). Part of the migration from each of these countries thus clearly flowed overseas. But if – as seems reasonable – migration to the United States can be taken as being tolerably representative of this trend, a second basic feature emerges. That is, the rate of migration to the United States from Wales between 1880 and 1910 was only half that from England and was an even smaller proportion of the flow from Scotland and Ireland.[4] The third aspect is that in the period from 1880 to the First World War most of the Welsh rural exodus stayed in Wales. Following earlier British studies which divided the country into Towns, Colliery Districts and the Rural Residue, Brinley Thomas demonstrated that in the 1880s and 1890s the number being absorbed into industrial south Wales was almost enough to absorb – statistically – the total rural exodus, and in the 1900s the number being absorbed was far greater than the numbers being released from the rural districts. This was in contrast to the 1860s and 1870s when most migrants from rural Wales could not be absorbed within Wales and thus left for England or overseas (A.15).

Brinley Thomas also provides a powerful and cogent economic explanation for the pattern which emerged. This need not be repeated here since the immediate concern is simply with the question of the destinations of those who moved from Welsh rural areas. From the 1800s they mostly stayed in Wales. There was always movement out – to England and to countries like the United States: but these had ceased to be the typical destinations. The movement was toward the southern coalfields

A.14

A.15

CENSUS OF ENGLAND AND WALES.
1881.

(43 & 44 Vict. c. 37.)

PRELIMINARY REPORT,

AND

T A B L E S

OF THE

POPULATION AND HOUSES

ENUMERATED IN

ENGLAND AND WALES,

AND IN

THE ISLANDS IN THE BRITISH SEAS,

On 4th April 1881.

Presented to both Houses of Parliament by Command of Her Majesty.

LONDON:
PRINTED BY GEORGE EDWARD EYRE AND WILLIAM SPOTTISWOODE,
PRINTERS TO THE QUEEN'S MOST EXCELLENT MAJESTY.
FOR HER MAJESTY'S STATIONERY OFFICE.

1881.

[C.—2955.]   *Price 1s. 6d.*

Pages from the Preliminary Report of the 1881 Census. (*Source: Glamorgan Archive Service.*)

unrevised and the revised totals of all England and Wales, with a population of nearly 23 millions, amounted at the census of 1871 to no more than 8,158.

The error was still more insignificant in respect to the number of inhabited houses ; for, out of a total of more than four millions and a quarter, the difference between the revised and the unrevised figures was but 85. The preliminary figures, therefore, may be used without fear for the larger divisions of the country, and still more for the country itself, and it is only in the case of the smaller sub-divisions, such as sub-districts, that caution is required.

The total number of persons returned as living in England and Wales at midnight on April 4th, 1881, was 25,968,286.

Total population of England and Wales on April 4, 1881.

This was an increase of 3,256,020, or of 14·34 per cent., upon the numbers living at the previous census of April 3rd, 1871, and was almost exactly equivalent to the addition of another London with all its inhabitants to the population.

The rate of increase was higher than in any decennium since 1831–41, when it was 14·52. In the two succeeding decades (1841–51 and 1851–61) the rate fell, first to 12·65 and then to 11·93 ; but in 1861–71 the rate again rose to 13·19, to be, as already noted, still further advanced to 14·34 in the ten years just completed.

The rate of increase in the aggregate population of England and Wales is almost entirely determined by two factors, namely, the birth-rate and the death-rate ; for, in comparison with these, emigration and immigration have but an insignificant effect. The rapid growth of the past decennium was due to the fact that the birth-rate was unusually high, while the death-rate was still more unusually low. That is to say, the additions were somewhat above the average, while the losses were far below it.

Causes of the high rate of increase.

	Mean Annual Birth-Rate.	Mean Annual Death-Rate.
1841–51	32·61	22·33
1851–61	34·15	22·25
1861–71	35·24	22·50
1871–81	35·35	21·27

The higher birth-rate in 1871–81, as compared with the preceding decade, implies the addition of 26,774 extra members to the community, while the lower death-rate implies the survival of 299,385 persons who with the previous rate of mortality would have died.

The difference between the total number of births and the total number of deaths in the ten years, or " the natural increment of the people," amounted to 3,425,982, or to an increase of 15·08 per cent. upon the population at the beginning of the period ; and as the actual increase, as determined by enumeration, was 14·34 per cent., the combined effects of all other movements of the population, including emigration and immigration, resulted in a loss of no more than 0·74 per cent. in the whole period.

The natural increment.

How closely the growth of the population is determined by the " natural increment," and in what small degree comparatively it is affected by other causes, is seen in the following table, which gives the population and the rate of increase for three successive decennial periods, as they would have been, if determined simply by the natural increment, and as they were found actually to be on enumeration :—

CENSUS YEARS.	POPULATION.		Difference of " Natural Increment " Population from " Enumerated " Population.	Increase per cent. in previous Decade.		Difference of Natural Increment Rate from Enumeration Rate.	CENSUS YEARS.
	As determined by " Natural Increment " only.	As actually enumerated.		As determined by " Natural Increment" only.	As determined by Actual Enumeration.		
1861	20,188,335	20,066,224	122,111	12·61	11·93	+0·68	1861
1871	22,791,234	22,712,266	78,968	13·58	13·19	+0·39	1871
1881	26,138,248	25,968,286	169,962	15·08	11·34	+0·74	1881

a 4

which were absorbing labour at a very high rate, especially in the 1900s, and also, more modestly, towards the growing holiday towns of north Wales.

The substantial population shifts which have been indicated naturally had far-reaching social, economic and political reper-cussions. They reflected the considerable change which took place in the economic structure of Wales. In economic terms this contributed to a general increase in income because it represented a move of resources away from low-productivity agriculture and towards higher-productivity industry.

In 1851, 35 per cent of all occupied males were engaged in agriculture: in 1911 only 12 per cent were so engaged. The absolute decline in the number occupied in agriculture was not all that great (from 135 to 96 thousands), but it meant that the industry had not been able to absorb the natural increase in the population which thus had to look for employment elsewhere. In the case of those counties which were primarily agricultural this usually meant leaving the county altogether. The transition of Wales from an agricultural to an industrial nation was effectively accomplished during these years. One of its con-sequences was that the population became, by 1911, much more concentrated around the south Wales coalfield, and around the slate quarries and smaller coalfield in north Wales.

One of the features most generally commented upon – both at the time and since – was that it was a process which involved rural depopulation. And so it did – of a sort. But it is important to be clear about the nature of this depopulation. Briefly it can be said to have had three broad characteristics: it was highly concentrated; it was limited; and it was most conspicuous as a relative phenomenon. Five counties[5] experienced some fall in the absolute level of their population in the half century or so before 1911 and these were, as already seen, mainly the counties in which agriculture was most important. Indeed, between 1881 and 1911 the actual decline was concentrated in only three counties – Cardigan, Merioneth and Montgomery – where the combined population fell from 188,000 to 157,500. The fall was by no means catastrophic. The total population of the five counties in 1881 had been 269,300 and in 1911 it was 240,500. But although the loss of rather less than 30,000 people over three decades cannot be seen as dramatic depopulation, it has to be given perspective in at least three broad ways. First, the late nineteenth century was simply the beginning of a long-run process. The movement from the land set in train an extended, creeping depopulation from, especially, rural mid-Wales. By 1971 the total population of the five counties had fallen to 205 thousands. The second necessary perspective is to view the population decline in these counties against the contemporaneous trends in other parts of Wales. In five of the most industrializing counties[6] the population increased between 1881 and 1911 by well over one million. The two counties of Monmouthshire and Glamorgan on their own accounted for nearly 800,000 of this increase. And finally, it needs to be noted that the rural population exodus affected a much higher proportion of the counties of Wales than of England and to a much more marked extent. Thus between 1881 and 1891 most (eight) Welsh counties suffered a population decline compared to only twelve of the English counties, and in five of the Welsh counties (mostly in mid-Wales) the percentage decline was greater than even the worst-affected English county (A.16).

A.16

The effect of the move from the land on the health and viability of the Welsh language has been much more controversial. For long the conventional wisdom was that it was part of a process which necessarily undermined the language. Welsh-speakers were being drained away from rural districts where the use of the language was most general and where it was most protected from outside influences. It was often an implicit assumption of this view that these Welsh-speakers emigrated to America or *Patagonia* or wherever. But that aspect was not ultimately essential since an even stronger assumption was that industrialization necessarily undermined the language and its mutually-supportive culture. This entrenched position, however, became untenable after it had been subjected to the decisive bombardment embodied in Brinley Thomas's seminal article on 'Wales and the Atlantic Economy'.[7] It was demonstrated, as already seen, that most of the Welsh migrants were able to stay in Wales and, moreover, Wales kept most of its natural increase in population. And all this was only possible because of the industrialization of Wales.[8] Thus the total number of Welsh-speakers in Wales was almost certainly higher than it had ever been before. And, it is argued, that this – despite the fact that they constituted a smaller proportion of the total population – 'gave the Welsh language a new lease of life' and 'a second chance' to establish itself (A.17).

A.17

There is no doubt that the Brinley Thomas arguments and evidence have permanently shifted the debate about the relationship of industrialism to Welsh culture: they cannot be shrugged off as being 'merely statistical'. Equally there are some obvious difficulties with the argument. Even in the earliest language censuses (1891, 1901, 1911) it is clear that the divide between areas of high and low proportions of Welsh-speakers was at least as much a west/east as a rural/ industrial phenomenon.[9] Of much greater significance are the implications of the scale of the inflow into the south Wales coalfield between, especially, 1901 and 1911. Prior to this the normal situation was that the net loss by migration from rural Wales was greater than the net gains of the colliery and urban areas. From the language and cultural view-point this meant that, whilst there was always some exodus to England or overseas, most of the Welsh natural increase stayed in Wales; it also meant that, whilst there was always an inflow from England, the non-Welsh migration into industrial south Wales was relatively modest and, in any event, tended to concentrate in the coastal ports and towns of east Wales. Each of these features made it possible to absorb and assimilate the non-Welsh element, especially in the Glamorgan valleys. And, to a degree, this does seem to have happened. But in the decade 1901–11 the position changed radically. The scale of the inflow into Monmouthshire and Glamorgan (nearly 130,000) far surpassed the *net loss* from rural Wales. From one point of view this reinforces the view that industrialization strengthened the language: all the movement of Welsh people from the land could have been absorbed (several times over) by the industrial expansion. The snag was in the 'several times over', for that meant that there was necessarily a huge influx of non-Welsh. This was on a scale (at least 100,000) and in a time-span (a single decade) that made absorption unlikely or impossible. In addition the huge growth of the mining labour force in this decade makes it clear that this particular tidal wave was not confined to the already strongly anglicized coastal ports of Newport and Cardiff and Barry.

Much of this has been recognized and, indeed, presented by Brinley Thomas in his latest work.[10] But it is still robustly maintained it was only the industrial revolution and economic growth which prevented the Welsh language (and people) going the same way as the Irish; that the million or so Welsh speakers at the end of the nineteenth century gave Welsh a second chance; and that, contrary to myth, the life and rigour of the culture was centred in industrial Wales and not in the so-called rural heartland. It is an issue that will continue to be debated but is not likely to be resolved because, like many aspects of the move from the land, it manifests itself in ways both immeasurable and imponderable.

A.18

Much the same might be said of the effects of emigration on social customs or the elusive, but significant, concept of the idea of the community (A.18). In part, therefore, judgements will necessarily be subjective and depend on how individuals respond to Goldsmith's assertion that

'A bold peasantry, its country's pride,
When once destroyed can never be supplied.'

Debates about the effects and seriousness of the move from the land, in other words, are conditioned by the extent to which one subscribes to some concept of a rural arcadia. Some people see rural life as having inherently superior values; others see it as having simply more space.

Notes

1. A. W. Ashby and I. L. Evans, *The Agriculture of Wales and Monmouthshire*, Cardiff, 1944.
2. H. Carter and S. Wheatley, *Merthyr Tydfil in 1841*, Cardiff, 1983.
3. See especially B. Thomas, 'The Migration of Labour into the Glamorganshire Coalfield, 1861–1911', *Economica*, X, 1930, and 'Wales and the Atlantic Economy', *Scottish Journal of Political Economy*, VI, 1959.
4. Brinley Thomas, 'Wales and the Atlantic Economy', ibid., Tables 1 and 3.
5. Breconshire (1861), Cardiganshire (1871), Merionethshire (1881), Montgomeryshire (1841) and Radnorshire (1841). The dates in brackets indicate for each county the census years at which the population was at its peak.
6. Carmarthenshire, Denbighshire, Flintshire, Glamorgan and Monmouthshire. The total population of these counties in 1881 was (in thousands) 839.9: in 1911 1,914.5. The combined totals of Glamorgan and Monmouthshire for the same years were 722.7 and 1,516.6.

7 Originally published in *Scottish Journal of Political Economy*, November 1959 and re-printed in B. Thomas (ed.), *The Welsh Economy*, Cardiff, 1962.

8 And also because the Welsh industrial economy was heavily export-based, which gave it a different cyclical pattern to that of the general British domestic economy. One result of this was that economic activity tended to be booming (and hence attracting migrants) at just those times when the overall British economy was most depressed (thus inducing people to migrate). But this more technical aspect – which

9 Anglesey, Caernarfon, Cardigan, Merioneth and Carmarthen each had about 9 per cent Welsh speakers at the turn of the century, but Caernarfon and Carmarthen each had a low proportion in agriculture by 1911. On the other hand three of the 'depopulating' rural counties of late nineteenth-century Wales – Brecon, Radnor and Montgomery – had a low proportion of Welsh speakers. It is interesting to note that another index of 'a Welsh way of life' or 'a Welsh culture' – voting on Sunday – closing of public houses – was still strongly west/east in the 1960s and early 1970s.

10 B. Thomas, 'The Industrial Revolution and the Welsh Language Revisited', in L. J. Williams and C. Baber (eds.), *Papers in Welsh Economic History*, Cardiff, 1984.

Sources

TABLE 1: POPULATION, WALES AND EACH COUNTY, 1851-1911 (000s)

	1851	1861	1871	1881	1891	1901	1911
Wales	1,163.1	1,280.4	1,412.6	1,571.8	1,771.5	2,012.9	2,420.9
Anglesey	57.3	54.6	51.0	51.4	50.1	50.6	50.9
Brecon	61.5	61.6	59.9	57.7	57.0	54.2	59.3
Caernarvon	87.9	95.7	106.1	119.3	118.2	125.6	125.0
Cardigan	70.8	72.2	73.4	70.3	62.6	61.1	59.9
Carmarthen	110.6	111.8	115.7	124.9	130.6	135.3	160.4
Denbigh	92.6	100.8	105.1	111.7	117.9	131.6	144.8
Flint	68.2	69.7	76.3	80.6	77.3	81.5	92.7
Glamorgan	231.8	317.8	397.9	511.4	687.2	859.9	1,120.9
Merioneth	38.8	39.0	46.6	52.0	49.2	48.9	45.6
Monmouth	157.4	174.6	195.4	211.3	252.4	298.1	395.7
Montgomery	67.3	66.9	67.6	65.7	58.0	54.9	53.1
Pembroke	94.1	96.3	92.0	91.8	89.1	87.8	90.0
Radnor	24.7	25.4	25.4	23.5	21.8	23.3	23.6

(Census Returns)

TABLE 2: NET GAIN (+) OR LOSS (−) BY MIGRATION

	1851		1861		1871		1881		1891		1901		1911	
	No. 000s	%	No. 000s	%	No. 000s	%	No. 000s	%	No. 000s	%	No. 000s	%	No. 000s	%
Wales	+9.1	+0.85	−19.8	−1.67	−49.5	−3.82	−52.1	−3.67	−17.8	−1.13	−9.4	−0.53	+98.5	+4.84
Anglesey	+1.2	+3.15	−5.0	−12.48	−5.0	−13.09	−2.4	−6.88	−3.2	−9.2	−1.5	−4.49	−1.9	−5.42
Brecon	−2.4	−4.27	−6.6	−11.18	−9.0	−15.27	−9.5	−16.64	−7.0	−12.85	−5.6	−10.32	−3.5	−6.53
Caernarvon	−2.5	−2.92	−4.5	−4.55	−2.6	−2.53	+1.2	+1.09	−8.5	−6.83	+2.8	+2.24	−4.9	−3.57
Cardigan	−9.4	−9.82	−9.3	−9.54	−10.2	−10.43	−11.3	−11.56	−15.7	−16.53	−7.3	−8.41	−3.7	−4.53
Carmarthen	−6.5	−7.23	−13.8	−14.60	−8.2	−8.52	−5.5	−5.38	−7.9	−7.07	−8.6	−7.30	+10.7	+8.63
Denbigh	+1.6	+1.69	+0.4	+0.38	−6.1	−6.16	−4.1	−3.91	−7.5	−6.60	−1.2	−1.07	−3.4	−2.65
Flint	−4.4	−10.79	−4.4	−10.67	−1.0	−2.45	−3.2	−7.37	−7.8	−17.04	−4.4	−10.26	+1.6	+2.60
Glamorgan	+41.9	+23.52	+44.2	+18.42	+19.0	+5.82	+30.3	+7.47	+77.5	+14.94	+41.0	+5.92	+92.1	+10.63
Merioneth	−4.2	−8.26	−2.8	−5.42	+1.7	+3.27	−1.5	−2.52	−10.7	−15.70	−5.2	−8.09	−8.4	−13.02
Monmouth	+9.6	+6.36	−6.1	−3.45	−7.2	−3.65	−21.7	−9.89	+3.7	+1.58	−5.1	−1.86	+34.4	+10.86
Montgomery	−7.6	−9.56	−7.3	−9.51	−6.6	−8.63	−11.1	−14.24	−15.8	−21.72	−8.7	−12.89	−6.6	−10.32
Pembroke	−4.7	−5.99	−5.7	−6.80	−13.8	−15.77	−9.4	−11.20	−11.6	−13.85	−7.2	−8.79	−5.5	−6.64
Radnor	−3.8	−11.81	−2.9	−9.19	−3.2	−15.07	−3.7	−18.78	−3.4	−18.48	+1.0	+6.06	−4.7	−23.16

(Calculated from Census Returns)

29

A.2   Radnor is included despite a net increase in 1891–1901 because, as the census remarks, 'At the date of the recent census, the population of the county was augmented by a large number of men temporarily engaged in the construction of new water-works for the corporation of Birmingham. These men, together with their families, account for the abnormal increase in the population of the county.'

(1901 *Census*, County tables, Radnor. Table 1, footnote).

A.3   PERCENTAGE OF OCCUPIED POPULATION ENGAGED IN AGRICULTURE

	Males			Females		
	1851	1881	1911	1851	1881	1911
Wales	35.3	20.4	11.9	26.8	6.9	9.4
Anglesey	49.2	39.6	39.5	34.9	11.4	27.9
Brecs.	40.8	35.7	23.9	26.2	5.4	12.9
Caerns.	39.4	23.6	19.2	28.4	6.4	8.8
Cards.	49.6	47.2	45.4	42.6	16.7	26.3
Carms.	46.2	29.5	21.3	38.0	12.7	21.3
Denbs.	44.9	26.7	21.6	27.8	6.3	10.9
Flints.	24.6	15.4	17.7	21.6	5.3	8.7
Glam.	15.4	6.0	2.5	13.1	2.1	2.0
Merioneths.	53.1	31.3	32.2	40.0	9.0	15.8
Mons.	21.0	12.7	5.7	13.0	2.6	3.3
Monts.	56.1	45.4	49.1	30.3	9.5	20.8
Pembs.	40.9	31.5	29.5	31.7	11.7	21.7
Radnor	63.7	56.9	52.6	39.4	5.0	13.5

(Calculated from Census Returns)

A.4   POPULATION IN AGRICULTURE (000s)
        NUMBER ENGAGED IN AGRICULTURE (000s)

	Males			Females		
	1851	1881	1911	1851	1881	1911
Wales	135.4	100.0	96.0	33.7	10.7	20.2
Anglesey	6.5	4.4	6.2	1.5	0.4	1.1
Brecs.	8.2	6.0	4.8	1.7	0.3	0.8
Caerns.	11.7	9.0	7.6	2.7	0.9	1.3
Cards.	13.5	11.7	7.9	4.9	2.3	2.6
Carms.	12.9	9.2	11.3	4.4	1.6	4.0
Denbs.	14.1	9.5	10.1	3.0	0.7	1.6
Flints.	3.2	2.2	5.2	0.7	0.2	0.8
Glam.	13.1	10.0	9.5	3.0	0.9	1.6
Merioneths.	8.5	6.8	4.7	2.2	0.6	0.9
Mons.	13.3	9.5	7.8	2.1	0.5	0.9
Monts.	14.3	10.8	8.5	3.0	0.8	1.5
Pembs.	9.7	7.6	8.3	3.3	1.2	2.5
Radnor	6.5	3.3	4.0	1.3	0.1	0.5

(Census Returns)

A.5   Mr Phillip Pennant, landowner, Flintshire, Chairman of
        Quarter Sessions: 'Yes, and the worst of it is that the best
        labourers have gone away. A clever man will see his way to
        better himself by going into the district where there are works
        and so forth, and they go and they leave the worst behind, so
        that there is no doubt that the labour has increased in price, and
        at the same time has deteriorated in quality.'

        (*Royal Commission on Land in Wales and Monmouthshire*, Evidence,
        Vol.IV, Q.57,272, 1896, c.8221, Vol.XVI).

A.6   Agricultural workers, by reason of the scattered and dispersed nature of their industry, have never succeeded in forming, or at least in keeping for long in effective existence, any trade unions for the purpose of securing a fair share in the profits of the industry. This seems to be the sole reason why they did not get a larger share in the good times during the thirty years before 1880. As it was they worked then and afterwards during the next thirty years of depression, for very long hours at very low wages. The workers had their full share in the good times, so far as concerns money wages. Indeed the bad times were best for them, because, while their wages remained about the same or were, if anything, rather higher, the cost of their articles of consumption went down, so that their real wages were higher than they had been before 1880.

(*Commission on Wages and Conditions of Employment in Agriculture*, 1919. General Report, para. 527).

A.7   The causes of rural depopulation have not altered in any significant way during the last century and a half. A change in emphasis has naturally occurred between the various factors involved, and both at different times and at different places the local or regional causes of the rural exodus will lay a different stress upon individual forces of expulsion. The basic cause is everywhere the same. Rural depopulation has occurred in the past century and a half, and will continue in the future, because of declining employment opportunities in the countryside. Economic activities have steadily moved from the villages and the rural communities into the towns and the urban areas; and as employment possibilities have diminished in the rural areas, the village populations have moved into the towns. To put the matter thus baldly is greatly to simplify a complicated problem, but it is nevertheless important to grasp hold of the basic elements of the rural problem. The historical forces that have been at work since the late eighteenth century have led to a concentration and a centralization of economic life in large industrial units and in large urban agglomerations and rural life and rural society have been steadily weakened. Without the provision of work there can be no reversal of the depopulating trends in our rural society.

(J. Saville, *Rural Depopulation in England and Wales, 1851–1951*, 1957).

A.8   No shortage of labour, despite emigration, except occasionally at hay harvest. 'Much assistance used to be given in former days in Wales by village artisans and small tradesmen with their families on all occasions of emergency at the neighbouring farms. But the number of country shoemakers and tailors, carpenters and blacksmiths, and small shopkeepers has greatly diminished with the growth of the tendency to buy both articles of apparel and of furniture 'ready made' as well as to get all provisions from stores in towns.'

Report on Poor Law of Narberth (Pembrokeshire and Carmarthenshire).

(*Royal Commission on Labour*. The Agricultural Labourer, Vol.II, Wales, 1893, p.60).

Moreover, during the last 50 years, many small industries that were carried on in rural districts, frequently as auxiliary to agricultural employment, tended to disappear. Sixty or seventy years ago most of the chief towns of Wales had some special industry of their own that gave employment to a large proportion of their inhabitants. Thus, hats were largely made at Carmarthen and Monmouth, boots at Narberth, Haverford-west, and Lampeter, and stockings, knitted gloves and caps (called Welsh wigs) at Bala: Amlwch had its tobacco manu-factories and Llanerchymedd was famous for snuff and boots. Most famous of all was Swansea for its porcelain and china, an industry which was also carried on at Nantgarw in another part of the county of Glamorgan. The town of Holywell was remarkable for activity in various manufactures, there being in 1831, 256 males, upwards of 20 years of age, employed in the manufacture of silk and cotton goods, in making paper, and manufacturing iron, copper, brass and lead. Mold, at the same time, had 230 men employed in the cotton manufacture.

(*Royal Commission on Land in Wales and Monmouthshire*, Report, 1896, p.45).

A.9 With these reservations I shall state boldly that I believe the main causes to be two, of which the one may be termed *sentimental*, the other *economic*.

(1) Whatever poets may have said of the pleasures of the country, whatever country squires may say in praise of turf or turnips, *burn* or moor, with whatever glee the jaded merchant or banker may rush off to the woods of Surrey or the dales of Cumberland, there can I think be no manner of doubt about the feelings of the great mass of the population. To them the country does not suggest pleasure, but the lack of it. The dream of the countryman is to get away from the country, just as it is the dream of many townsmen to get away from the town. Change naturally enough is attractive to us all, but whereas it is almost the rule for the rustic to wish to go to a town, it is comparatively exceptional for the townsman to wish to leave one.

I believe this, which I have called the sentimental cause, to lie at the very root of the matter, but it is, all said and done, of the nature of what medical men term *predisposing causes*; we have now to consider the *existing cause*.

(2) This, which I believe will be found in some form or another to underlie those various contributory causes – which, in one case and another, may be so much more *in evidence* as to seem at first sight to be the chief cause – has many forms, and acts in many ways. It may be summed up in the phrase *improved communications*. See what this implies. In the first place, the man who wants to go finds the means of transit. In the last century locomotion was slow, inconvenient, and expensive. It is now rapid, handy, and cheap. Improved communications include cheap postage and cheap telegraphs, which render possible a cheap press. These in their turn have had much to do with the spread of education. The press and the post put the village in communication with the town, the factory, the mine, the colonies. Men learn where there is a demand for labour, and are directed to it. Improved communications lead to the central-isation of industry; this in its turn lessens the demand for artisans in the country, while it increases the demand for them in the towns.

(Longstaff, 'Rural Depopulation', *Journal of the Royal Statistical Society*, 1893, pp.413–14).

A.10   Thus, in Wales machinery has not replaced manual labour to the same extent as it might have been expected. In many cases it has made possible a more thorough cultivation, which in turn has necessitated an increase in labourers. Whenever a large decrease has taken place it is attributable not so much to a change in the method of farming as to a change in the very nature of the agriculture pursued – the substitution of stock grazing for cultivation.

(*Royal Commission on Labour*, Agriculture Labour Wales. Report of Leufer Thomas, 1893, p.7).

A.11   The attractions of farm life were said to be especially strong for young girls. '. . . Perhaps also town life has a greater fascination for them than for the men. The number of country girls . . . who go in for dressmaking is astounding, and one often wonders if half their number get any work at all. Welsh girls are also in great demand as domestic servants in England, owing to their character for industry, honesty, and cleanliness, partly the result of an early religious training, and partly (in many cases) of a bringing up on a small holding where a taste for work has been acquired . . . '

'The watering and other tourist centres in North Wales are often the means of drawing good girls from the farms, leaving inferior men behind. In their new stations they get good wages, a large amount of gratuities and presents from visitors, and what is sometimes more appreciated, a lively, albeit a hard time during the continuance of the short season. The best girls are almost invariably taken to England by the visitors and in time are the means of inducing others to follow in their wake.'

(*Royal Commission on Labour*. The Agricultural Labourer, Vol.II, Wales, 1893, p.11).

A.12   In addition to those competing industries within Wales which have attracted so many labourers from farm work, large numbers have migrated from Wales to the United States of America – probably Montgomeryshire has provided more emigrants than any other agricultural county. During the great *Mormon* propaganda of some 30 or 40 years ago hundreds of men left the districts of Wick and St Bride's Major in the south of Glamorgan for *Salt Lake City*. A Welsh agricultural colony founded in 1863 at Chupat in the Argentine Republic has also drafted from Wales a small portion of the rural population, but Canada and other agricultural colonies have not proved very attractive fields of emigration for Welsh labourers.

(*Royal Commission on Labour*. The Agricultural Labourer, Vol.II, Wales, pp.20–21).

For a time *S.R.* *(Samuel Roberts)* sought a solution of all the problems of the Welsh peasant in emigration. Throughout the century a constant stream of emigrants had left Wales, settling, almost without exception, in the United States of America. There, the land-hunger of generations of Welsh peasants was at last satisfied. *S.R.* adopted the idea of *Morgan John Rhys*, half a century earlier, and sought to settle the Welsh together in a community. So, in 1856, he purchased 100,000 acres of land in eastern Tennessee, and a party of emigrants set out under the leadership of his brother. *S.R.* himself followed with another party in the spring of 1857. But the experiment was a failure.

(D. Williams, *A History of Modern Wales*, 1950, pp.257–60).

A.13 A few remarks may, however, be made as to the chief centres and districts where Welshmen are found congregated in England. And first as to London. The number of persons actually born in Wales and enumerated in the London Registration District in 1891 was returned as 31,292, while it has been estimated that there were also 14,828 natives of Wales resident in the outlying districts. Thus in West Ham alone (which is outside the boundary of the Registration District of London) there were 961, Willesden 529, Tottenham 329, and Leyton 259, while a little further afield we find 856 returned as resident to Croydon. Mr Thomas Darlington has estimated that out of a total of 46,120 natives of Wales resident in London and outlying districts (in 1891), as many as 23,954 were able to speak Welsh. At all events, we have the fact that religious services are conducted in Welsh every Sunday at about 40 different centres in London.

As compared with the resident population enumerated in each of the Welsh counties, we find that the proportion of their natives settled in London is much higher for Cardiganshire than for any other county. Omitting nearly 5,000 Welsh-born London residents, the county of whose birth was not stated, we find that a number equivalent to 5.25 per cent of the total population of Cardiganshire had migrated from that county to and were settled in London, 3.5 per cent from Pembrokeshire, about 3 per cent from Radnorshire and Montgomeryshire, and 2 per cent from Breconshire. The remaining counties of north Wales are represented by a number equivalent to about 1 per cent of the population enumerated at home. Monmouthshire and Carmarthenshire have 1.7 and 1.4 respectively, while Glamorganshire comes last with 0.8 per cent. The most interesting point about this is that it is the agricultural counties (more especially of south and mid Wales) that, in proportion to their home population, send the largest number of persons to settle in London. The comparative paucity of north Walians is due to the fact that north Wales comes more within the sphere of influence of Liverpool than of London, and that the former town therefore stands for many purposes in the position of a capital for north Wales, whence there is ready access not only by rail but by water also. In a lesser degree and of more recent years Manchester has begun to compete with Liverpool in this respect.

We can make but a very rapid survey of the distribution of the natives of Wales in the provincial towns of England. In the chief towns of Lancashire and Cheshire they are to be counted by the thousand. Liverpool in 1891 had 17,449 persons born in Wales, Birkenhead 5,654, and St Helen's 1,393. The number in Manchester was 6,764 and in Salford 2,699. The total number of persons born in Wales and enumerated in Lancashire amounted to 60,819, while the neighbouring county of Cheshire had 21,379. But these figures give a very inadequate idea of the total Welsh population of these towns. Thus, as the result of a special inquiry conducted by Mr Thomas Darlington in connection with the Welsh congregations of Manchester, it was estimated that 25 per cent of the 'hearers' at these churches had been born outside Wales, and would therefore not be included in the figures quoted above from the Census. The proportion of Welshmen resident in Liverpool but born outside the Principality is stated to be much greater than in Manchester.

(*Royal Commission on Land in Wales*, 1896, Report, pp.57–8).

A.14   WALES, ENGLAND, SCOTLAND, IRELAND, SWEDEN, AND USA: RATE OF NET LOSS (−) OR GAIN (+) BY MIGRATION, DECENNIALLY, 1851–1911

Period	Wales	England	Scotland	Ireland		Sweden	USA
				North	South		
	Annual rate per 10,000 mean population						
1851-61	− 28	− 16	− 101	− 194		− 7	+ 98
1861-71	− 47	− 7	− 44	− 169		− 37	+ 67
1871-81	− 35	− 5	− 28	− 119	− 127	− 32	+ 51
1881-91	− 11	− 23	− 58	− 108	− 163	− 74	+ 80
1891-1901	− 5	− 2	− 13	− 55	− 118	− 37	+ 37
1901-11	+ 45	− 19	− 57	− 52	− 82	− 36	+ 63

(B. Thomas, 'Wales and the Atlantic Economy', reprinted in B. Thomas (ed.), *The Welsh Economy*, Cardiff, 1962, p.7).

A.15   WALES: INTERNAL MIGRATION, DECENNIALLY, 1851-1911
NET LOSS BY MIGRATION (−). NET GAIN BY MIGRATION (+)

Area	1851-61	1861-71	1871-81	1881-91	1891-1901	1901-11
Welsh rural areas	− 63,322	− 53,967	− 64,646	− 106,087	− 57,413	− 37,909
Glamorgan-Monmouthshire colliery areas	+ 39,627	+ 11,033	+ 12,213	+ 87,225	+ 40,326	+ 129,295
Wrexham colliery area	+ 2,661	− 1,934	− 1,907	− 1,122	− 618	− 2,875
Llandudno and Rhyl areas	+ 1,259	− 2,263	+ 2,339	+ 2,190	+ 8,289	+ 5,715
Wales	− 36,271	− 63,005	− 52,139	− 17,794	− 9,350	+ 98,492

(B. Thomas, 'Wales and the Atlantic Economy', reprinted in B. Thomas (ed.), *The Welsh Economy*, Cardiff, 1962, p.15).

A.16　If, however, we take the counties separately, and at the same time compare the results with those obtained in English counties, we find that if placed in the order of their decrease (in population between 1881 and 1891) they would stand as follows:

	per cent
Montgomeryshire	11.68
Cardiganshire	9.20
Radnorshire	7.58
Flintshire	7.01
Merionethshire	5.81
Pembrokeshire	3.59
Brecknockshire	3.44
Anglesey	2.57
Huntingdonshire	5.51
Herefordshire	5.18
North Riding of Yorkshire	4.62
Shropshire	4.39
Lincolnshire	4.29
Rutlandshire	3.84
Cornwall	3.76

It thus appears that it is in the Welsh counties that the rural depopulation has assumed the most notable proportions, and with the Welsh counties may be classed the border counties of Herefordshire and Shropshire.

(*Royal Commission on Land in Wales*, 1896, Report, p.47).

A.17　Instead of bemoaning the rural exodus, the Welsh patriot should sing the praises of industrial development. In that tremendous half-century before the First World War, economic growth in Wales was so vigorous that her *net loss* of people by emigration was a mere 4 per cent of her bountiful natural increase over the period. Few countries in Europe came anywhere near to that.

(B. Thomas, *op.cit.*, p.28).

A.18   The *neithior*, or bidding, was in effect and among other things a customary form of savings club. A man (or woman) started to contribute sums of money or make contributions in kind during his teens, he 'drew on the club' on marriage, and continued to pay into it for the rest of his life, both in order to repay contributions he had received on his marriage and in order to claim repayment on behalf of his children when they came to marry. David Davies of Penalltygwin in Troedyraur parish, and later of Galltycnydie in Llangynllo parish (where he was farming in 1849), gave 'An Account of the Weddings which I David Davies has been since I were born'; he had then been to 102 biddings and his wife to seventy-one. Another David Davies of Tan y ffynnon, near Llwynrhydowen in South Cardiganshire, either attended or contributed to 154 biddings during the nineteenth century. Here then was an institution that involved a man for most of his life with a large number of his fellows, and which provided for one of the critical periods in any family cycle, establishing people upon marriage. And as farmers' children had to delay their marriages until there was sufficient provision to establish them, the bidding allowed of earlier marriages than would have been the case otherwise. Further the bidding contributed to integrating individuals into a community for it gave people particular interest in the marriages and relationships of others, and a knowledge of their family histories, for it was on important occasions in these families' histories that bidding dues were rendered.

By the late nineteenth century the bidding was in decline and the reasons for this are complex. The bidding was then a changing institutionalized procedure within a society that was itself in process of change. One of the relevant general changes may be noted, namely, emigration to the industrial areas of south Wales and elsewhere and a partial replacement of the emigrants by people without any prior connection with the area. The bidding depended on the repayments of debts over a lifetime by people who had contracted them on one occasion and on the making of contributions by those who expected to claim repayment either on their own behalf or on the behalf of people who were their 'near relatives'. But once continued emigration made it uncertain whether a young man would remain in his native area or emigrate he was in no position to know whether he would be in a position to reclaim against any contribution that he had made, nor would others know whether debts owing to them would be repaid by people who might emigrate. There are indications that emigration was affecting certain of the institutions of South Cardiganshire by the 1870s. Until that decade farm servants were hired at the annual hiring fairs at Newcastle Emlyn, Cardigan, and other centres; during the 1870s it became common practice to hire in advance of the fairs because there was a shortage of servants as the result of emigration. The fair increasingly became a pleasure fair while the hiring of servants was undertaken independently. In the same period it became the practice to send 'industrial school-boys' into south-west Wales to be employed as farm servants as an insufficient number of local youths was available. These industrial schoolboys had no place in the area as members of kin groups nor was there any certainty that they would remain in the area. Thus the conditions upon which the bidding depended, that there were people who tied themselves for a lifetime expecting that their future would be spent in the same general area, were rendered uncertain and for this reason among others the bidding declined. When this happened there was no longer any institutionalized provision, involving some hundreds of people, for establishing people on marriage, and the whole burden fell on the individual families concerned. In the depressed conditions of the closing years of the nineteenth century many farmers felt themselves obliged to delay their children's marriages as they could not spare the live and dead stock that would be required to help set them up on farms of their own.

(D. Jenkins, *The Agricultural Community of South-West Wales at the turn of the Twentieth Century*, Cardiff 1971, pp. 134–5).

The recorders' notebooks of the census of 1861 show that 54 per cent of the residents of Troedyraur parish had been born in the parish, the birthplaces of a further 27 per cent were in adjoining parishes, and of a further 9 per cent in neighbouring (not adjoining) parishes, a total of 90 per cent. By 1861 the population was already declining. The population of the agricultural areas of South Cardiganshire generally reached its maximum during the 1840s excepting only where there were woollen mills. From that time on migration more than balanced the natural increase. On the other hand immigration into the rural areas of South Cardiganshire was on a very limited scale until the Second World War and the years following so that the proportion of the population which had been born in the area remained high, being virtually identical with those of forty years earlier.

Thus individuals grew up knowing other people as the fathers, mothers, brothers, and sisters of their school friends and neighbours. In later life they would come to know youngsters as the children and grandchildren, cousins, nephews, and nieces of those with whom they grew up together. That is they grew up with a knowledge of 'who people were' in a locality rather than needed to acquire such knowledge *in toto* by deliberate effort as they would were they to emigrate to a strange community. And the knowledge of people in a community rather than a systematic genealogical knowledge of kin as such.

(D. Jenkins, *op.cit.*, pp.158–9).

Debating the Evidence

One of the objectives of this book is to present as wide a range of historical evidence as possible. To a considerable extent this has been achieved in the first set of documents relating to John Williams's essay on the nature and significance of migration from rural to industrial Wales around the turn of the nineteenth and twentieth centuries. He has constructed a variety of tables from census returns, he has used Royal Commission evidence extensively and, interestingly, specialist and generalist secondary sources. Here is a reminder already, then, that primary sources are not the only ones of value to the historian. Both primary and secondary sources need to be treated rigorously and critically. There is often a misapprehension among people who are not historians that in some sense primary sources are 'true' and secondary sources are biased. It is vital to remember that *all* historical sources have

Dockers unloading pit wood, Barry, *c.*1911. (*Source: Welsh Industrial and Maritime Museum.*)

some element of bias. Among the objectives of the exercises and discussion which follow is to highlight elements of bias in the sources.

Source A.1 Table 1

Q.1 Are census returns *necessarily* reliable? What would you need to know about them before deciding on whether the returns in this Table are reliable?

Q.2 On the basis of these figures what generalizations can you make about the population of Wales in the period being studied? What of the *distribution* of population across Wales in this period?

Source A.1 Table 2

In the light of the further information provided in Table 2 how would you modify the generalizations you made in response to Table 1? Why?

Sources A.3 and A.4

These Tables provide information about agriculture in the Welsh counties. If you were studying (a) Welsh politics, (b) the history of the Welsh language, are there any ways in which these figures might be useful to you?

Source A.5

As you see, the evidence cited here has been given to a Royal Commission. We can be sure that within very narrow limits the evidence given has been accurately recorded. Does this mean that the information is reliable?

Sources A.6 and A.7

Are these primary or secondary sources? A.7 was written relatively recently. Are its conclusions compatible with those in A.6? How would you describe the difference of approach and tone in these sources to the topic of rural depopulation?

Source A.8

What possible reasons *might* there be why there was 'no shortage of labour, despite emigration . . .', apart from the one given in the document?

Source A.9

Is there any difference *in kind* between what the writer calls 'sentimental' evidence and 'economic' evidence, as these are set out in this document?

Source A.10

Does this information modify in any way your thinking about Source A.8?

Source A.11

Comment on the *strengths* and *weaknesses* of this Source as a starting point for investigating the history of women in late-Victorian Wales.

Source A.12

Why should Montgomeryshire provide so many emigrants to the USA?

Source A.13

What other kinds of information would you need to have about Welsh people in English cities before being able to assess their role and impact in these cities? From the information which is given here do any *patterns* of emigration and settlement suggest themselves?

Source A.14

How might the information reproduced here help the historian of (a) religion in Wales (b) the Welsh language?

Source A.17

Do you detect any evidence of bias in this document?

Source A.18

The book from which these quotations are taken is an excellent book based on impeccable research. On what basis do you think I am able to make these statements?

Discussion

You will all be familiar with the dismissive phrase 'lies, damned lies and statistics'. On the face of it this sentiment seems very odd. If you count the number of people in a room, or a tutorial class, or a cinema, or a county, and record the number accurately, this surely has more objectivity than recording, for example, that the people in the room were 'calm', or 'only there for the beer'. Ascribing motives to a large group of people is inevitably partial since the variables are probably as great as the number of individuals involved.

To take the example of the cinema crowd, it would seem to be objective evidence if we had a record of the number of people who actually attended on a particular evening and such evidence would be readily available, because there would be checks on the number of people who paid for tickets (of course even this would not be totally accurate, since some people might have been given complimentary tickets). It would certainly be subjective evidence to ascribe motives to those going to the cinema. Even the trite observation that they went to see the film might well not be true for the courting couples occupying the back row. There is an element of truth in the notion that statistics, accurately recorded, are objective. However, the historian's questions are inevitably going to be complex ones, even about cinema-going. The worthwhile activity comes in the interpretation of the statistics, to indicate, for example, that cinema-going is on the decline because of, say, the advent of television. Once *that* proposition is made, the statistics are put in perspective. The statistics provide vital information, the essential base, but the interpretations which can be put on them are as varied as with any other information.

In his essay John Williams has shown just how complex the interpretation of statistical information can be, how subtle the reasoning which deduces certain social consequences from the raw data of population figures. What we must remember, however, is that there is a stage before this. The census data which he uses must be subjected to the tests of validity and reliability essential in dealing with all historical documents. The historian's approach must be sceptical. He should accept nothing at face value. It is *possible* that John Williams might be desperate to prove a thesis about movement of population in Wales. He could have invented the figures presented here to suit a predetermined case. But this is where the historical apparatus of footnoting and listing of sources in bibliographies comes in. He tells us that these figures are taken from the census returns for the relevant years. We can go to a major library and check the figures in the table against the printed compilations of figures in the relevant census reports. We are now an important stage further on, but we still have to ask whether the printed census reports are accurate. We must ask how *they* were obtained. The techniques by which the information was obtained are set out in the reports and they indicate a high degree of accuracy for such relatively recent censuses. However, it is well to remember that we cannot get beyond this. The census enumerator's returns, on which the printed census reports are based, do exist, but they are not available to researchers until 100 years have elapsed. Still, this does allow access to the enumerator's returns for 1881.

Having considered the way in which the source came into being, and concluded that the statistics provided are accurate within narrow limits, the author and his readers need to reflect on whether those limits have an effect on the kinds of questions which the essay poses. John Williams's arguments are not actually affected by the limitations in the accuracy of the statistics. He does not require figures accurate down to the last individual. He is pointing to *trends* for which percentages are perfectly acceptable. As historians we can now rest content that the author's figures are sufficiently accurate for his purpose. What he *makes* of those figures, his interpretation of them, is, of course, a matter on which he has to convince you and me – his readers.

At the opposite end of the spectrum the author also quotes from secondary sources. Sources such as A.12, part 2, can provide us with new information or a new perspective. But even a cursory look at David Williams's information on *Samuel Roberts*, Llanbryn-mair, indicates some of the problems encountered with all general texts. What are we to make of such phrases as 'almost without exception', 'the land hunger of generations of Welsh peasants was at last satisfied', 'the experiment was a failure'? Where might we start with interpreting the reliability of *this* passage? First, we have made the most important of steps in identifying generalizations which *may* be suspect. Even when we are reading the work of a historian as accomplished as the late David Williams we must be on our guard for judgements of this kind. David Williams's book, *A History of Modern Wales*, is a textbook for sixth formers and undergraduates and does not carry footnotes. However, it would not be difficult to build up a short bibliography of monographs and articles which would deal with the work of *Samuel Roberts*. The obvious place to start here is with the *Dictionary of Welsh Biography*. We are on our way to doing a piece of research. Ultimately, that is the only way we can illuminate historians' generalizations.

Wales at Work

DAVID EGAN

There is no point in work
unless it absorbs you
like an absorbing game
when a man goes out into his work
he is alive like a tree in spring
he is living, not merely working.

D. H. Lawrence, 'Work' from *The Complete Poems*

The effect, value and importance of work in people's lives is a
crucial but complex question for the historian. In the setting of a
society such as Wales during this period, answers to the various
questions which we might wish to ask about the experience and
influence of work require rigorous and sympathetic treatment
of historical sources which are imperfect and fragmentary.
Although the growth of what is known as 'oral history' (the
tape-recording of the testimony of those who lived through a
period of the past) is making a valuable contribution to our
understanding of the life of common people, we still have to
recognize what Alisdair Clayre has called the 'silence of the past'
which stems from the plain fact that working people rarely leave
behind them the kind of personal evidence which would be so
valuable in investigating this question. It is in the nature of the
historian's own work-skills that he has to labour within such
constraints and perhaps one particular skill is called for in this
context: it is that of *empathy* – the ability to enter into the secret
world of the past and, free of as many as possible of our own
values and preconceptions, to understand that world as it was

Women hauliers at Abergorki Colliery, Treorchy, *c.*1880. (*Source: Cyril Batstone.*)

lived in. This essay sets out to argue that for too long historians have been bereft of this skill in their approach to the question of work and that it is only through more sensitive treatment of the sources that clearer understanding is emerging.

A fundamental starting point when considering work experience in Wales during this period is the marked extent to which work did absorb people's lives. This resulted from the fact that compared to our own time people started work earlier in life, worked longer into old age, spent more time at work, had greater opportunities for employment and were more 'involved' in work through the dominance of 'hand' over 'machine' work. What is also striking is that this took place against the background of a vibrant Welsh economy undergoing a rate of growth which on a world scale was only matched by the Eastern United States of America and the Ruhr coalfield in Germany. Agriculture was an exception to this overall pattern as the combined effects of a market depression and the lure of alternative employment in rapidly expanding industries produced a decrease of male agricultural wage earners of 45.7 per cent and a 94.9 per cent fall in female labour, between 1851 and 1911. By 1911 only 10.06 per cent of the adult male workforce was employed in agriculture and thus in less than a lifetime the traditional way of life and employment in Wales had been eroded. In marked contrast, the growth of extractive and manufacturing industries in Wales during this period was phenomenal. By 1914 the coal industry of south Wales dominated the world export market and employed 234,000 workers – nearly one quarter of the whole adult male population. In metal manufacture the old iron industry was in the process of giving way to the new technologies of steel production and therefore it was tinplate production which was dominant, employing in 1911 a workforce of 21,000 (including the largest group of women employed in manufacturing) and dominating world production of tinplate from its concentrated base along the coast of south-west Wales, which also was the home of the major producers of copper, brass, zinc and nickel. In north-west Wales slate quarrying reigned supreme, employing 14,000 workers in the 1880s and boasting the largest slate quarry and mine in the world as the industry expanded rapidly until a slump began before the First World War. Transport industries such as the railways and the docks also prospered as they met the needs of this markedly export-directed expansion and 85,481 workers were employed in this sector by 1911. An even more significant expansion in employment occurred in domestic services where female labour was dominant and this is an area of work experience where our knowledge is as yet sketchy and provisional.

In considering work experience within this strident economy the traditional approach of historians (particularly economic historians) has been to concentrate on what they regarded as the essence of work — labour carried out for periods of time within certain working conditions and rewarded by the payment of wages. Working hours were long, particularly so in agriculture, the working week was extended, and it has to be remembered that holidays were few (B.1, B.5, B.9, B.12). Whilst it is true that in most areas of employment hours and days of work had been or were being shortened, nevertheless the extent to which life was dominated by work is clear.

B.1
B.5
B.9
B.12

Conditions of work can also be seen to have been oppressive (B.1, B.5, B.6, B.10). Work in agriculture, quarrying and coalmining was physically hard and arduous (B.3, B.5, B.6, B.10). In all three work was often done in wet conditions and in the two extractive industries dust was another unpleasant factor. Mining and quarrying were excessively dangerous occupations as is made clear — below-ground dangers were ever present and the south Wales coalfield had the highest death rate in British mines between 1901 and 1910 with 1.78 of every 1,000 workers being killed; quarrying was no less dangerous, whether above or below ground, due to work on high galleries where explosives were used to free huge slabs of rock. The question of wages is a notoriously difficult one for historians to deal with. In the case of agriculture it is complicated by wide regional variations, *payments in kind* (rent-free cottages, food, for example), different methods of payment for different workers, the availability of additional seasonal work and so forth. In the coalmining and the tinplate industries some of the same factors defy firm conclusions — *piece work* dominated here and as in other industries such as slate quarrying (where the '*bargain*

B.1
B.3
B.5
B.6
B.10

system' operated), and on the docks and railways (where the casual nature of employment further complicated matters) wide variations in what workers actually received in wages make averages and single examples only a little more meaningful. There is also the fact, of course, that wage rates are a very different thing from actual earnings and even more importantly those earnings can only be truly gauged when purchasing power is also taken into consideration. This whole area is a minefield of interpretation in relation to working with evidence and it is therefore not surprising that the general conclusion which historians usually come to is that if workers were forming trades unions and carrying out collective action in the way they were increasingly doing during this period over wages questions, then wages must have been regarded as unsatisfactory.

Indeterminate as we may have to be over the question of wages, it does, however, bring us to terms with what, it will be argued here, is the severe limitation of measuring work experience solely by the indices of average hours, general conditions and average wages – lives were not lived in 'averages' nor is experience illustrated by those indices which historians have dizzily constructed. The example of wages will suffice to make the point clearer. For agricultural workers it might be the quality of the food offered at a particular farm or the way in which a farmer cared for his horses, which influenced a labourer in deciding whether to accept a place or not. For the piece-work collier the decision whether to increase output and thereby wages, appears to have been often overborne by the desire to reduce work intensity, to increase leisure hours and to ensure sufficient safety conditions. The docker clinging to the casual system which reduced his wage-earning potential, the quarryman forgoing the more rewarding contract system so as to keep control of his work through the cherished '*bargain*' – they all point to a view of work very different from the purely economic values which the historian has often imposed upon the past.

If we begin to exercise the skill of empathy we can see that for those who spent so long at work it was necessary to create a world *within* work which involved values of people's own choosing. Status within work was highly prized by the agricultural labourers who became servants at the farms and thus, if they were men, worked with horses, which was regarded as 'the highest work' compared to the cottagers who carried out general tasks such as hedging, ditching and draining. Even amongst the cottagers (or 'general labourers') work distinction was important: despite the fact that milk brought in a farm's main cash income the job of cowman was regarded as 'the lowest work' as it was thought degrading for a man to milk and it was therefore consigned to labourers who were too old for any other work.

Although, as will be argued below, skill at work was also an important factor, it was not the only determinant of status within agricultural work as the case of piece-workers shows. This type of labourer was regarded as possessing a great degree and variety of skills, yet in the eyes of the community was placed at the bottom of the hierarchy of status which derived from work. Slate-quarrymen were equally concerned about status, both compared to other groups of workers (they regarded themselves as of a higher status than the agricultural workers who surrounded them in Caernarfon and Merioneth) and within the quarry workforce. Only something like one half of those who worked within a quarry were the actual crew of quarrymen who worked, *split* and *dressed* the slates. The rest of the workforce was made up of *bad-rockmen*, *rubbish-men*, time workers and *rybelwrs*, who in effect were young men learning the quarryman's skill. Although the actual quarrymen earned little more than the others they regarded themselves and were so regarded, as the elite due to the particular skills which they possessed. In the colliery exactly the same type of status-gradation operated: the skill of the repairer, the haulier, the *farrier* was highly regarded but it was the experienced collier who was accepted as the 'aristocrat' of the mine. It is important to note, finally, that this status which derived from work emanated from the accepted values of a community or at least a community of work and often contradicted the categorizations drawn up by 'official society' in the sense of census returns or government departments. Official attitudes viewed the craftsmen (the carpenter, blacksmith or engineer) as superior to the farm servant or collier – the 'community' did not.

The question of skill has already received comment and this brings us to pride in work, which again is a value that has been underestimated in traditional approaches to the study of work. In the countryside the pride in work which servants derived from working with horses led to them purchasing brasses from their own wages and, on some occasions, totally disregarding those wages. Should a farmer decide to sell their particular horse, servants responded by ending their contract with the farmer. The agricultural community as a whole viewed itself as a highly-skilled society and a premium was put on the quality and variety of skills which even the general labourer was expected to have in the tasks of cultivation. Great expertise in a variety of skills was required of the quarryman who, in the words of R. M. Jones, 'with gunpowder, and crowbars, hammer and chisel, and skill, blasted and coaxed the slate from the mountain'. It was accepted that the nature of slate rock could only be gathered from long training and experience and that a true 'quarryman' should be able to carry out the winning of the slate, its *splitting* and its *dressing*. When it came to variety of skills no worker was more of a 'jack of all trades' than the collier, who was expected to master the skills of *roofing, cutting bottom*, drilling holes for explosives, ensuring ventilation and many other complex tasks as well as the actual winning of the coal. Similarly, in the tinplate industry, skills were viewed as almost an inherited quality, particularly as the high degree of geographical concentration of the industry in the Swansea and Llanelli areas made the industry virtually a family concern. The ambition of anyone who entered as a *'behinder'* was to proceed via a long apprenticeship to the position of *Rollerman*. Even in what many people regarded as the lowest type of labouring – casual work in the south Wales ports – skill as a 'ship' or 'shore' worker, and among shore workers, as a *coal trimmer* or timber porter, was prized. Status followed and was treasured despite the fact that these divisions often worked against the men as they reduced their mobility and thereby their chances of employment. Pride in skills and in work was, then, a factor of considerable importance to those who toiled in harsh and often brutalizing conditions, but, nevertheless, created their own standards of the

B.1 value of the labourers (B.1, B.4, B.7, B.8, B.9, B.11, B.12).
B.4 In agriculture it was to a large extent the control which
B.7 labourers exercised over their work which enabled pride to be
B.8 taken and, again, work control is an area which needs careful
B.9 appreciation in relation to work experience during the period.
B.11 In farming, the fact that servants would leave the employment
B.12 of a farmer if he took his own horse without the permission
of the head servant, the very existence of piece-workers who
'bucked' the traditional life of being tied to a farm as a servant
or cottager, and the way in which pride in work was measured
not by any standards set by the farmer but by one's accepted
equals or peers, are all indicative of the extent to which control
of work was valued. In slate-quarrying the great strikes and
lock-outs of 1874, 1885, 1896–7 and 1900–3 were in essence
disputes over the right the quarrymen claimed to control their
own work and the determination of the owners and managers to
wrest that right from their workforce so that they could manage
their own concerns. The quarrymen recognized that they did
not own the quarries but they did believe that it was their right
to control the hours they worked, the days they worked, the
methods they used to perform their skill and the system they
worked and were paid under. The idea that managers, who had
risen through the quarry office and not through quarry *work*,
could dictate to them was something they firmly rejected and
this issue was ranked far more highly than the money they were
actually paid. The collier rejected the idea of supervision and
management in exactly the same way, for he too was the master
of his work situation as he supervised and was responsible for
his own methods of working. Often where the *'butty system'*
persisted, and always where a 'boy' worked at his side, the
collier took responsibility for the work of those other than
himself. The industrial struggles of the south Wales coalfield,
particularly during the 'labour unrest' immediately before
1914, are nothing less than the resistance of a workforce
which felt threatened by subjugation by the new coal combines
which attempted, as the quarry-owners had done before them,
to take control of the industries they owned. Colliers, like
the quarrymen, knew how to control output in a way which did
not necessarily enable them to earn higher wages but

maintained what they saw as something every bit as important
– the control of their work and thereby a large part of their
lives. The *Rollerman*'s control of the whole work crew
and the quality of the finished product in the tinplate industry,
and the attempt by foremen in the docks to control entry into
employment are also, in their different ways, illustrative
of the determination of a whole workforce in Wales during
this period to defend industrial democracy in an age before
workers realized they had lost it (B.1, B.3, B.8, B.9, B.10,
B.12).

Limitation of space precludes detailed comment on the extent
to which experience of work pervaded and influenced the rest of
people's lives, such as it was, given the domination work
exercised upon them (B.5, B.10, B.12, B.13). In agriculture the
mutual interdependence of a workforce which, during times
such as harvest, created an atmosphere of companionship,
shared endeavour and pride in attainment, extended itself to
frame a whole pattern of social behaviour in which, as David
Jenkins has pointed out, 'the maintenance of good relations was
an end in itself' because quarrels could have a serious effect on
work and were therefore to be avoided at all cost. In both slate-
quarrying and coal mining it is apparent that much of the reason
for workers turning to trade unionism after initially being
laggardly in their commitment was the threat posed by owners
to their control of the work situation. Consequently the *North
Wales Quarrymen's Union* and the *South Wales Miners' Federation*,
became an institutionalization of employees' attitudes to work
and thereby took on the form of organizations which were
much more than the means of improving wages and conditions
of employment. Men who worked in an environment of mutual
support and collective solidarity chose – whether through
choirs or trade unions – to express themselves similarly away
from work.

Living as we do in an age where the introduction of
machinery means that there are more tractors than agricultural
labourers in the countryside of Wales and where the mining of
coal by hand is left to be illustrated only by museums, we need
not be reminded that the nature of work has changed and with
this change have disappeared the relationships which stemmed

B.1
B.3
B.8
B.9
B.10
B.5
B.10
B.12
B.12

from work and framed the existence of life in Wales between 1880 and 1914. Within that society work was the life-blood of human experience and, therefore, its meaning and worth have to be measured not only by the wages which were earned or the conditions which were endured but also by capturing the total and absorbing effect which work had on people's lives and beliefs. As David Jenkins has observed of the agricultural labourers of south-west Wales, people 'would not have that time back if they could, but they are proud to have lived in it'. If we, as historians, wish to understand how that pride could have existed, we need to perfect *our* skills as *we* labour with sources which, however imperfect, are all that we have by way of entry into a lost experience.

Sources

B.1   The condition of engagements are generally from the 10th of October for the current year with so much per week, with cottages for married men. The hours of work are about 75 hours per week, made up as follows: we are supposed to be in the

Haulier driving a tram at a south Wales colliery, *c.*1905. (*Source: Welsh Industrial and Maritime Museum.*)

stable at 5.30 am to feed the horses and cattle, then home to breakfast, which takes up half an hour, and at noon we are supposed to get 1½ hours, but do not do so as the food for the horses and cattle have to be provided in this time, so that we have very little time for rest. We leave the field at night at 6 o'clock, but against we get home and do up the team for the night it is 7 o'clock; and it takes 3 hours for Sundays. This is from November to May – slightly less during the summer up to haymaking and harvest, when we work up to 8 or 9 o'clock often. Current wages for previous year was from 10s 6d to 12s 6d per week with cottage; we get no *piece work* nor do we request it as there is no time.

(Evidence of labourers at St Ishmael's, Haverfordwest Union; *Royal Commission on Labour*; The Agricultural Labourer: Vol.II, Wales, 1893, p.71).

B.2 Edward Jones, farm labourer, wife and five children, wages 16s; extra harvest and job work, 2s, equal to 18s.

Rent	1s 3d
Flour, 28lb	3s 0d
Tea, ½lb	0s 11d
Sugar, 6lb	1s 3d
Bacon and lard	2s 2d
Potatoes	0s 2d
Milk	0s 3d
Coal	0s 10d
Wood (gratis)	—
Butter	2s 2d
Salt, pepper etc	0s 1d
Soap	0s 4d
Club money	0s 6d
Clothing	3s 9d
Butcher's meat	1s 0d
Total	17s 8d

The man lives in a good cottage and garden; he is close to big woods and can get plenty of wood gratis; also he gets his potatoes by paying so much per *bushel* for planting in the farmer's field, and milk for six months in the year gratis.

(Labourer's budget in the Builth district.
Royal Commission on Labour; The Agricultural Labourer, Vol.II, Wales, 1893, p.174).

B.3   The piece-work men or jobbers are a distinct class by themselves, who do not care to hire themselves for the usual term of service . . . These are generally the most skilled among the labourers. The following are the prices that are paid . . .

Hay cutting	4s an acre
Singling roots	11s 6d to 13s per acre
Pulling roots	7s 6d and 8s per acre
Sheep shearing	1½d each for small sheep ⎫ with
	2d each for big sheep ⎭ food
Moving new bank of earth	2s 6d to 3s 6d a rood
Clearing ditch and banking side of fence	4d per rood
Clearing ditch simply	2d per rood
Draining (drain 2ft deep)	6d to 7d per rood
Draining (drain 2½ft deep)	8d to 9d per rood
Making new wall of loose stones (for fence) 4ft high	4s a rood
Making new wall, 1½ feet of it plastered	7s a rood
Mole-catching	2d a head, 2d an acre, or 2s a day and food
Cutting thistles	4d to 6d an acre
Thorn trimming and raking up trimmings	2d a rood

N.B. The rood is 8 linear yards.

(*Royal Commission on Labour*; The Agricultural Labourer; Vol.II, Wales, 1893, p.131)

B.4   They (the labourers) show great zeal in the management of their horses, and will steal from the master's granary to keep them in

A *Doubler* at work at the Clayton Tinplate Works, Glamorgan, *c.*1920. (*Source: Welsh Industrial and Maritime Museum.*)

good condition. They are said to choose places from the character which a farmer bears for keeping his horses well. It is the same with farming. Men will tell you within five miles who has got the best put in drills of potatoes or turnips, and whose barley field has been laid down in the most husbandlike manner. They will lose money rather than make a bad job of a hedge if it is within sight of a road.

(Commissioners Report on the Poor Law Union of Builth. *Royal Commission on Labour*; The Agricultural Labourer: Vol.II, Wales, 1893, p.165).

B.5   *Cerdd yr Hen Chwarelwr*

Hogyn dengmlwydd gerddodd ryw ben bore,
Lawer dydd yn ôl, i gwr y gwaith;
Gobaith fflachiai yn ei lygaid gleision
Olau dengmlwydd i'r dyfodol maith.

Cryf oedd calon hen y glas glogwyni,
Cryfach oedd ei ebill ef a'i ddur;
Chwyddodd gyfoeth gwr yr aur a'r faenol
O'i enillion prin a'i fynych gur.

Canodd yn y cor a gadd y wobr,
Gwyddai deithiau gwyr y llwybrau blin;
Carodd ferch y bryniau, ac fe'i cafodd,
Magodd gewri'r bryniau ar ei lin.

Neithiwr daeth tri gwr o'r gwaith yn gynnar,
Semwyd am y graig yn torri'n ddwy;
Dygwyd rhywun hua'r ty ar elor,
Segur fydd y run a'r morthwl mwy.

(*The Old Quarryman's Ballad*

Early one morn, many a long day past,
A boy of ten on his way to work departed;
And in his blue eyes hope was cast
As a boy often saw his future start.
Stony at heart were those blue rock faces,
But mightier still were his *auger* and iron
Thus, he increased the wealth of the man of means and fine places
Through his meagre earnings and frequent pain.

He sang in the choir which won the prize,
He knew the tiring paths the men trudged,
He courted a girl from the hills to make her his own
And on his knees giants of these hills were nurtured.
Early, last evening, three men from the work came there
For the rock, so they said had cleaved in two,
And someone was brought towards the house on a bier –
So from now on, that chisel and hammer will be silent too.)

(W. J. Gruffydd, *Caneuon a Cherddi*, 1906).

B.6   I do not think the public fully realize that one out of every six or
seven of all the boys and men employed in the industry, surface
and underground, every year get ignored to an extent that
renders them idle for at least seven days – and large numbers of

them are totally and permanently disabled. This is an occupation in which men are blown to pieces. Only recently I had to deal with a compensation claim for two young men, the only sons of parents, who were both killed instantaneously. I have seen a father, a son-in-law, and four sons who all left the house hale and hearty in the morning, brought back in the evening charred corpses, and no one left in the home but the two widows, mother and daughter. The only difference between the soldier and the miner is that the miner can never ask for an armistice. He cannot even treat for terms of surrender. The casualties go on every day.

(Evidence of Vernon Hartshorn, Miners' Agent, South Wales Miners' Federation, to the Coal Industry Commission, 1919. *Reports and Minutes of Evidence on the First Stage of the Enquiry*, pp.362-3).

B.7 *Average Earnings of Full-time Tinplate Workers in South Wales, Monmouthshire and Gloucestershire, 1906*

Furnacemen working at piece rate	47s 3d
Rollers	62s 10d
Doublers	50s 10d
Behinders	26s 9d
Shearers	61s
Annealers	41s 11d
Tinmen	43s 6d
Assorters	50s 5d
Boxers	45s 1d
General Labourers working at day rate ..	22s 9d

(*Report of an Enquiry by the Board of Trade into the Earnings and Hours of Labour of Workpeople in the United Kingdom*, 1911, p.56, Cd. 5814).

B.8 Revised List of Prices, Big Vein

Cutting and filling of Large Coal	2s 4d per ton
Cutting and filling of Thro' Coal	0s 10d per ton
Cutting and filling of small coal	0s 2d per ton
Narrow places not over three yards wide	3s 0d per yard

Stalls between three and five yards wide	5*d* per yard
Machines incline between three and five yards wide	4*s* 7*d* per yard
Double timbers (not notched) in *stalls* and airways	1*s* 6*d* per yard
Props and Posts in Upper and Lower Sides Only	6*d* each
Cogs in Upper Side of Roads	3*s* 0*d* each
Cogs in Lower Side and in *Gob*	2*s* 0*d* each

All Double Timbers in Levels to be put up by Company unless otherwise arranged.

Clod 1/- per inch per yard to be paid for.

Clod in narrow pieces up to and including five yards wide. A double measurement to be made or 2*s* per inch per yard to be paid in places over five yards wide.

(Section of Price List issued by Great Mountain Anthracite Collieries Company Limited, January, 1894. South Wales Miners' Library, University College of Swansea).

The Puddling Furnace, Cwmbran Ironworks, from the original oil painting in the Department of Industry, National Museum of Wales. (*Source: Welsh Industrial and Maritime Museum.*)

B.9   It all had to be cut then by the pick . . . Sometimes if you had a pretty active roof and there was an amount of subsidence the coal would crush and it would be easy to mine, and your chief worry would be the control of the roof. But other times you would have to hole it or undercut it. You would lie on your side and hack away and hole it under as much as a yard. And then there were various methods of getting it down, sometimes you would have to *sprag* . . . it and then you would withdraw the *sprags* . . . and eventually you would hear grumps and crackings and it would fall. Otherwise you would have to drill a hole and put gunpowder in or use clamps and wedges . . . coal-cutting in those days was a very skilled operation . . . the actual working of the fourteen yards of face would be done by the collier. There was a fireman who would come in at about 4 o'clock and make an examination for gas . . . and the overman who was respons-ible for output would come around any odd time . . . 7 o'clock was the alleged starting time for the pit but the men would come in anything up to nine . . . it was common for those men afterwards to be there until eight and nine in the night see.

(W. H. Taylor of Blaenavon interviewed in 1973 about his working experience at Blaenavon Colliery prior to 1914. Transcript, South Wales Miners' Library, University College of Swansea).

B.10   The immediate cause of the outbreak in October, 1900, was the following: For some time previously a system of big contracts, let to one man, had been brought into the quarry, which in the opinion of the men, was a great injustice to a large class of workers. An inferior class of workmen took these contracts, and engaged a superior class of men to work under at reduced prices. In October last 14 men were engaged on a part of Fridd *Ponc*; two of the men were placed to do a certain job by the day; they were engaged on Thursday and Friday, and had not finished; the following day was pay day, and, as such, a short day, but the under agent told them that they would have finished next day, and it was most unfair to keep them on the job on the Thursday and Friday, and take them off it the next day because it was a short day. The men did not work on the Saturday, and the 14 were suspended for three days. In about a fortnight the 14 were informed that they were not to be allowed to work in the same district any more, but were to be distributed to various parts of the quarry, and in the meantime all their bargains were let in one contract to one of the big contractors, against whom there had been growing great enmity. When this man with four of his workmen came on the *Ponc* and began work, the man of the poncs above him . . . eventually led him out of the quarry . . . on the 18th December, 1900 . . . the deputation (of the men) asked Mr. Young (the manager) for the following concessions:

1. The right freely to elect spokesmen from the ranks of the men in the quarry to discuss grievances with the management from time to time.
2. The right of the men during the dinner hour to discuss matters among themselves in the quarry.
3. The reinstatement of certain victimised leaders.
4. The establishment of a minimum wage.
5. The punishment of unjustifiable conduct on the part of foremen and officials towards the men.
6. The introduction, experimentally, of a system of co-operative piece-work in place of work hitherto done under contract.
7. The humanising of the harsh rules of discipline, and the reduction of the punishments for breaches of them.
8. The reintroduction of the annual holiday on May 1st.
9. More democratic control of the Quarry Sick Club.

(W. J. Parry, *The Penrhyn Lock-Out 1900–1901*, London, 1901, cited in I. D. Thomas, *Datblygiad Mudiad Yr Undebau Llafur Yng Nghymru*, Cardiff, 1975, p.32).

B.11   Slate quarrying is not a matter of mere manual labour but an art which years of patient practice will hardly require a . . . *slate splitter* is like a poet . . . and contends with the poet on an equal footing at the National Eisteddfod where *slate-splitting*, music and poetry are stock subjects of rivalry.

(*Pall Mall Gazette*, 1885. Quoted in R. M. Jones, *The North Wales Quarrymen*, Cardiff, 1981, p.74).

Slate splitting, Dinorwig Quarries, *c.*1910. (*Source: Gwynedd Archive Service*)

B.12   It was in the Wythien Fach at Betws Colliery that I started work
as a collier's lad in 1904. I was sponsored by my brother, Shoni,
to become the second boy to his big mate, Shoni Cardi. The
order of the day ran as follows. Call from mother at 5.45am,
then don the uniform of Welsh blue flannel shirt and drawers,
moleskin trousers and an old coat with big pockets sewn inside
to hold the food box and the water jack; a hasty breakfast and on
to the road to reach the pit by 6.15am; then on the spoke and
down the slant and on to the double-parting and a halt to attend
the Miners' Spell, time for the eyes to adjust to the darkness.
This was the Colliers' Parliament, where all the issues of the day
were discussed . . . Having put the world to rights, onto the
coal-face and the day's work. The Wythien Fach (Little Vein)
was two feet seven inches thick and the *stall* would measure
three yards, with seven yards on the top side of the face and five
yards on the lower. There was a steep inclination in the seam
and this added to the burden of the collier's boy, whose job it
was to gather the coal, cut by his mate, into the curling box and
carry it to the tram . . . The collier boy had to be careful to pick

only the lumps of coal, as the piece work collier was only paid for the large coal in the tram. The tram would hold up to thirty hundredweight of coal, and when it was full it was the boy's responsibility to mark the tram, with chalk, with the collier's number and then the number of the tram as filled during the fortnight from one pay to another.

The hours of work at that time were from seven in the morning to half past four in the afternoon, and in the winter months we would see daylight only on Saturday afternoon, when we finished at 1pm, and on Sundays. The boy's starting wage was 1*s* 3*d* per shift, plus the added percentage, and the total came to 1*s* 7*d* . . . At eighteen years of age, having served five years apprenticeship, I joined with another of my age to work our own *stall* on shares . . . The pits remained small, employing from a hundred up to five hundred workmen. The owners of these small mines knew each other intimately; they not only worked in the same mine, but also lived in the same village, attended the same chapel or frequented the same 'locals'!

(J. Griffiths, 'The Miners' Union in the Anthracite Coalfield', G. A. Hughes (ed.), *Men of No Property*, 1971, pp.60-61).

B.13   The condition of the miners' work naturally tends to make them responsible to a call for unity. They work under a constant sense of danger and of dependence on each other. Every man realizes that he may have to appeal at anytime to his mate for help and that his mate may have to cry to him. No man can live as an isolated individual – all are bound together by a sense of mutual dependence. This all has a great influence when their ideas are expressed in a wider field such as trade unionism.

(Extract from manuscript written by anonymous Pontardawe Miner, in Thomas Jones Papers, University College of North Wales, Bangor, Library: Ms. 4562).

Debating the Evidence

After having consulted the documents for the first essay we are now familiar with some of the kinds of sources used. Once more there is statistical evidence and material from Royal Commission reports. There are, additionally, two particularly interesting new types of source. There is poetry and there is oral history. In studying questions on the sources relating to David Egan's essay we will need to bear in mind some of the special problems posed by these potentially valuable but difficult types of source.

Source B.1

What more would you like to know about the labourers who gave this evidence before making use of the documents?

Sources B.2 and B.3

Part of the 'unwitting testimony' or 'unintentional record' of these documents is that in 1894 central government was interested in the wages and rates of pay of farm labourers. What reasons might there be for this?

Source B.5

On the basis of this poem of W. J. Gruffydd's, what do you think are the advantages and disadvantages of poetry as a source for the study of history? For what kind of purpose might you use poetry? What would you like to know about the *poet* before using this source if you were studying the history of the North Wales quarrymen at the turn of the century?

Source B.6

From the information at your disposal how reliable do you think this document is? What *other* evidence would you like to have before using this extract?

Source B.7

Compare the evidence in this document with that in document B.2. Just on the basis of the information in these two documents what generalizations could you make about conditions in rural and industrial Wales?

Sources B.9 and B.10

Compare and contrast these documents as historical evidence. What further information would you ideally like to have available before answering the question?

Source B.11

What, if anything, would you like to know about the *Pall Mall Gazette* before using the evidence for the study of the North Wales quarrymen?

Sources B.12 and B.13

How far does the evidence in the second of these documents support that in the first? Would the fact that Jim Griffiths had gone on to be a cabinet minister in the intervening period influence your view of document B.12?

Hand milking at Felin Newydd, Cardigan, *c.*1900. (*Source: Welsh Folk Museum.*)

Discussion

Documents B.1, B.2, B.3 and B.4 serve as a useful reminder of the vital distinction in historical research between intentional and unintentional record or, as another historian has it, witting and unwitting testimony. Royal Commission reports abound for the nineteenth century and the accumulated factual information is a goldmine for historians, particularly social historians. The 1893 Royal Commission on labour is of central importance in providing the raw material for David Egan to use in his essay. However, the report also testifies, unwittingly, to official concern at the time about labourers and their lives. These extracts show that evidence was taken from labourers themselves, something which did not happen in all reports which concerned them. There is unwitting evidence in the extracts that their conditions of work, hours and wages were sufficiently important to form part of the subject of a Royal Commission. That is only the start of a historian's investigation. Of course, this unwitting testimony merely leads him to ask why there should be this interest and to try to correlate it with contemporary political, economic and social concerns. Yet its importance is that it has sparked off questions which may lead to a fruitful and highly significant historical analysis.

Similar considerations apply with, for example, documents B.7 and B.8. Why should another official report be required in 1911 to investigate workers' earnings and hours of work? It comes to mind that David Smith's essay deals with the Tonypandy riots in 1910–11, and that these were symptomatic of unrest in many areas and industries before the First World War. Is there any correlation? There would be considerable work to do before the answer to this question could be provided, if indeed it ever could. The point at this stage is that unwitting evidence is vital in sparking off the kinds of questions which we need to address in order to interpret the significance of the intentional record in the source.

The distinction between witting and unwitting testimony is also of signal use in assessing the worth of literary evidence. W. J. Gruffydd was one of Wales's most outstanding poet-scholars, one of a number produced by the quarrying districts of north-west Wales, that area of Wales which has remained the most linguistically Welsh to this day. It is important to bear in mind that poetry does not serve the same purpose for the historian, as historian, as it does for the literary scholar. The historian looks to poetry to provide intentional and unintentional record like all his sources. The intentional information conveyed in this poem is limited, as it is in all poetry. The poet's function in modern times is seldom to set to verse some kind of record of the past. In this the modern poet's social function is distinct from that of the bards of, say, medieval Wales who were patronised by the princes and whose role in the household entourage was to recount the prestigious deeds of the prince and his forebears. The change in the poet's social function in the modern period does not mean that he is no longer of use to the historian. One excellent example here is the light which the theme and style of different genres of war poetry shed on attitudes towards the slaughter of 1914–18. So, we do not look to W. J. Gruffydd for factual information on the quarrying craft, or about the tools which the quarrymen used. This information might arise incidentally, but it would be easier to look it up in reference books on quarrying. What Gruffydd does incomparably is to illuminate the spirit of the place and time and fashion of quarrying work. In sixteen short lines here, we have summed up for us much of what quarrying meant to the individuals and communities of Bethesda or Corris or Blaenau Ffestiniog.

The wagon shop, Rhymney Railway Locomotive Works, Caerphilly, *c.*1906. (*Source: E. R. Mountford.*)

David Egan uses one further kind of evidence which merits separate comment. Oral history is one of the oldest and one of the newest forms of history. The bards of medieval Wales passed on their lore and tradition orally but the invention of the printing press was eventually to end all that. Historical fashions were such in the nineteenth and early twentieth centuries that the newly crafted method of the historian concentrated on rigorous application to the printed word in search of a dynastic interpretation of history –kings and queens reigned for the historian, too. In the twentieth century with increasing stress on social history it has become essential to rescue the evidence of those in society least likely to write down their life histories, but who have actually done the work or, less often, indulged in a variety of leisure activities and generally participated in the events which historians were busily interpreting without much reference to them. In Wales the most important project to rescue this mass of material has resulted in a vast amount of taped evidence being housed in the South Wales Miners' Library in University College, Swansea. David Egan worked on that project and here uses the fruits of his labour. However, there are snags. We now have two 'biases' to contend with, that of the interviewer and that of the interviewee. Many of these events are being recollected fifty years afterwards. What does *that* do to the memory? So oral history, in a particularly heightened form, serves as a reminder of the riches of the evidence available to the historians and the pitfalls to be negotiated in using it.

Language, Religion, Culture

TIM WILLIAMS

To study the history of late Victorian and Edwardian Wales is to be confronted with complexity and conflict. Whilst all societies are intricate and divided, Wales in this period was fractured, and for many of its inhabitants bewildering, the explosive growth of the iron and coal industries having blasted it out of its rural continuum into an unmapped modernity. This was unfamiliar terrain.

C.1 Into the unknown territory of south Wales poured men and women driven by the deprivations and hardships of rural life, and attracted by the possibilities of urban life (C.1). Against a background of dynamic economic growth and increasing intervention by the State, they developed practices, institutions and forms of association which might allow them to comprehend and order their own lives in a wholly new environment.

Thus it was that by 1914 Wales was impregnated with agencies of self-organization and amusement, in contrast to the early nineteenth century when religion, the public house and seasonal fairs were virtually the sole social outlets. Rugby clubs, choral societies, brass bands, trade unions, the working men's clubs and the *Workers' Educational Association* were some of the fruits of this process. So were the theatres, music halls, cinemas and sports arenas to which, in the south especially, a prosperous C.2 people flocked – much to the chagrin of the pious (C.2).

Once we as historians grasp that this process was neither inevitable nor unchallenged, being greeted with as much C.3 anxiety (C.3) as satisfaction, then the inter-relationship and importance of apparently quite separate activities become more obvious. They were areas of struggle and conflict over power and social initiative in the new society – and who was to possess it. To investigate cultural history is a fundamental, rather than a marginal, enterprise, as fundamental as the history of the economy or of politics with which we are more familiar, and with which the history of culture is so inextricably linked. This I hope to show by concentrating on the contentious issues of language and religion – prime sites of struggle over communication, leisure time and social participation in the new Welsh society of our period.

LANGUAGE

Late nineteenth-century Wales was bilingual. As early as 1891, the year of the first census of population to supply (contested) information on the Welsh language, only 54.4 per cent of the people of Wales could speak their native tongue (C.4). And only a minority of these were Welsh *monoglots*. By 1901 fully 84 per cent of the population is recorded as being able to speak English. Of course, the figures vary from region to region and, indeed, from generation to generation, with the highest percentages of Welsh bilinguals and *monoglots* being found in the counties of lowest population density, and the lowest percentages being found in the areas of highest population density. But only one county, Merioneth, registered a small majority of Welsh *monoglots* in 1901. The conclusion is inescapable: English was not a foreign language to most of the Welsh (C.5).

They do not seem to have been concerned, and this has been regretted by commentators who, intoxicated by a particularly dubious form of psycho-history, claim that the Welsh were suffering from an inferiority complex induced by the brainwashing habitually indulged in by state schools, which supplemented their symbolic violence towards the Welsh language by meting out physical punishment to its speakers. This assessment is both condescending and wrong (C.6).

In the first place, the chronology is unsatisfactory. State education was inaugurated in 1870, made compulsory in 1880 and free in 1891. In addition, Wales secured a separate *Intermediate Education Act* in 1889 providing for the extension of education beyond the elementary state: by 1902 there were 95

C.4

C.5

C.6

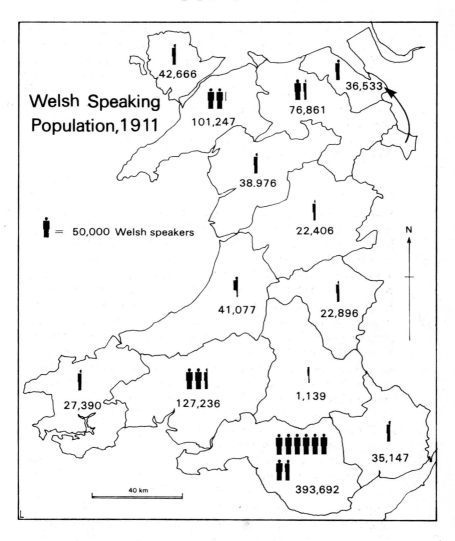

Welsh Speaking
Population, 1911

= 50,000 Welsh speakers

42,666

101,247

76,861

36,533

38.976

22,406

41,077

22,896

27,390

127,236

1,139

35,147

393,692

40 km

N

'County' schools in existence, inspected and examined by the *Central Welsh Board*. One of the problems with seeing this apparatus as a linguistic 'murder machine' is that, by 1901, a large majority of those too old to have come under the influence of the new educational system could speak English. Thus, 80 per cent of those in the 45 to 64 years bracket spoke English. Anglicization therefore preceded state-schooling (indeed, on the Welsh border, with very few exceptions, by a very long

C.7
C.8
time) (C.7) and was not dependent upon it (C.8).

Secondly, state schools, responsible after 1907 to the new *Welsh Department of the Board of Education*, were considerably more sympathetic to the Welsh language than those they replaced which had been paid for out of the pennies of the parents. The latter had no place for Welsh in their curriculum, whereas the *Welsh Department*'s civil servants were indefatigable in their attempts to give it a prominent position in school life, often leading them to be in advance of opinion in Wales on this

C.9
question (C.9). Crucially, whilst evidence as to the use of the

Examples of the 'Welsh Not'. (*Source: Welsh Folk Museum.*)

infamous '*Welsh Not*', hung around the neck of a pupil as a humiliation for speaking Welsh in the classroom, though scarce, can be found for the private venture or denominational schools, it is virtually non-existent for the schools of the Imperial British government.

To search for villains or victims in the process of linguistic transition is, in the last resort, unhelpful. It exaggerates the influence of institutions like schools – the example of Ireland suggests that languages can neither be killed nor resuscitated by means of schooling alone. It leads us to ignore the impact of impersonal forces on the one hand, and the capacities of majorities to resist oppression when they feel their interests to be at stake, on the other.

One of those 'impersonal forces' was the insatiable demand for workers in the labour-intensive coalfield of south Wales. This was temporarily met by migrants from other parts of Wales, mainly the counties bordering the area. Fleetingly, this massive movement of people created a Welsh-speaking industrial labour force, with the resources to support sophisticated and costly Welsh-language publishing ventures of a sort unrealistic in rural societies. That is, the Welsh, through industrialization, were colonizing their own country. Thereby they avoided the usual fate of rural minorities in the nineteenth century: emigration and the marginalization of their language.

The moment passed. King Coal's demands for labour could not be satisfied by the reserves of the area covered by the coalfield or the border counties. For example, from the 1870s, approximately half of the migrants to Glamorgan were coming from non-border counties, 37 per cent of the total making the journey from the agricultural districts of western and southern England – Cornwall, Devon, Somerset and Gloucester. Immigration was urged on by the boom in south Wales and the rural depression surrounding it. Further, the fact that the *Sliding Scale* for the payment of miners kept extraction costs low discouraged the introduction of labour-saving technology. So the influx of people spiralled upwards during the 1880s. By 1891, almost 40 per cent, over 260,00 people, had been born outside Glamorgan: 63 per cent of immigrants came from non-border areas, with Somerset providing the largest number from any county, at 11,900. Immigration slowed a little in the 1890s, but the climax of the expansion of the coalfield, 1901–14, brought a record flow of migrants, most of them English. In 1911, 239,064 of Glamorgan's population of 1,120,810 had been born outside Wales, equivalent to 24 per cent of males and 19 per cent of females. Moreover, over half the population was either born outside Wales or born to at least one non-Welsh parent.

C.10 The consequences for the maintenance of the Welsh language were dramatic (C.10). In 1891, 80 per cent of Glamorgan's population were Welsh, but only 49 per cent of them could speak the language. In 1901 this number fell to 44 per cent, only seven in every hundred being *monoglot*. By 1911 only 38 per cent were recorded as being able to speak the native language, with the Welsh-speaking population increasingly concentrated in the older age-groups.

In 1901, Anglesey was subject to the same educational system as Glamorgan – state-supported schools governed by elected Boards manned by the Welsh middle classes. Those who could speak Welsh constituted nine-tenths of the island's population. Immigration largely accounts for the difference between the two counties. Directly, it raised the proportion of the non-indigenous in society. Indirectly, it added to the difficulties of transmitting the language from one generation to the next in a context in which one's neighbours, schoolfriends, drinking partners, team-mates, colleagues, comrades, lovers – in a

C.11 phrase, civil society – might speak another (C.11). That language, increasingly in this period, was English. Especially for the young, who were the largest constituency in this new world where less than 5 per cent of the population was over the age of 65, English was the language of out-of-school activity

C.12 (C.12).

However, minority languages have survived in the face of great difficulties, even tyranny, where the collective will has been exhibited to sustain them. Why did Welsh shrivel in the air of freedom?

If coercion is discounted, what of deference? Perhaps the Welsh lacked confidence in themselves and their language or suffered from a defective national consciousness fostered by the 'ideological apparatus' of the British state? This does not seem to be supported by the evidence. Apart from the fact that the idea that there exists a 'proper' national consciousness is highly dubious, the people of Wales are hardly famed for either their deference or diffidence in this era. School *log-books*, newspapers, denominational journals, Government inquiries and police files all bear witness to the difficulties of attempting to control the inhabitants of the towns of the new Wales (C.13). The phrase, 'the problem of South Wales', coined at this time, conveys an awareness of failure in this endeavour. Moreover, opposition to the *Boer War*, the escalation of working class militancy, the school strikes of 1911 and the coalfield stoppage of 1915 indicate the limited capacity of the State to inculcate passivity in reluctant citizens. Quite simply, a gap always exists between intentions and effects in any process of communication, and it cannot be stressed enough that in a complex capitalist society, people are not blank slates upon which institutions can write at will without provoking struggle or contest.

C.13

To take part in that struggle, the Welsh chose English, the language of an Empire, certainly, but the language also of emerging democracy (C.14). A growing number of influential intellectuals, politicians and civil servants were committed to evolving a new consensus of the value of Welsh, both as expressive of nationality and as a spiritual tool in the fight against materialism (C.15). The state allowed them to do this. Apart from this, the attitude of the Welsh seems to have been one of indifference to the fate of the language, although the evidence for this has sometimes been suppressed (C.16). It could be argued that they showed a sensible understanding of necessary change.

C.14

C.15

C.16

RELIGION

Change was also overtaking that other conventional barometer of Welshness, religion, often conceived of as the opiate of the Welsh masses in this period. In fact religion was neither as neutralizing nor as all-embracing as we might think.

Reliable and objective statistics are difficult to obtain for the period 1880–1914, as denominations sought to maintain their share of the religious market by inflating membership figures. However, it is clear that a large majority of practising Christians in Wales, perhaps 75 per cent, frequented Nonconformist places of worship. But were the Welsh a nation of Nonconformists? In numerical terms, the answer must be that they were not, for if we add the significant and growing numbers of Anglicans to those who entered neither church nor chapel, then a clear majority of the Welsh people could not have been Nonconformists. But what of the influence of Nonconformity: surely this was more pervasive than the figures, inadequate as they are, might suggest?

To resolve this issue, and properly discuss the significance of Nonconformity, it is necessary to dispense with two notions. Firstly, Wales in this period was not some sort of theocracy, a closed, God-centred society over which *Dissenting* clergy exercised absolute and unchallenged command or 'social control'. Second, the chapel was not a purely theological domain. Only by clearing this ground can we build on firm foundations.

There is a tendency among some historians to see, let us say, the working class, as the study of the forces acting upon the working class. This has led some historians to assume successful control from above and ignore resistance from below. And how does the system achieve this conflict-free state? By means of institutions like the chapel, it is claimed. An adequate history of Welsh Nonconformity cannot be written from this perspective.

The fundamental reason for this is that the control imputed to Nonconformity has proved difficult enough to achieve in a totalitarian society, and impossible outside one. Also, by 1900 the Welsh environment was one in which the possibilities for leisure-time activity proliferated as incomes rose and working hours decreased. Nonconformity became, by 1900, merely one voice among many, clamouring – often in the columns of a commercial press dependent as much upon reporting boxing matches as on castigating irreligion – for the attention of an increasingly selective populace. Nonconformity responded contradictorily, often anxiously and sometimes hysterically, to this situation with different sects proposing different strategies. It did not control the situation (C.17).

C.17

How could it have? Through what mechanism? By means of what combination of force and fraud might it have enforced its moral diktats? It might advocate total abstinence, but could not prevent *Tory* magistrates from granting licences to public houses, or even some of its middle-class adherents from partaking of aperitifs in the privacy of their own homes. It might rail against street gambling, but could not compel the police to eradicate it. It might secure a legal ban on Sunday drinking in 1881, but it could not succeed in actually preventing drinking on a Sunday, and its attempts to do so, and to impose a general sabbatarianism, provoked opposition and rancour (C.18). It sanctified pre-marital chastity and the institution of marriage, and then saw those ideals mocked by immorality, illegitimacy and prostitution (C.19). It was appalled at what it saw as the licentiousness to be found in the miners' monthly holiday, *Mabon's Day*, but the latter's existence and abolition were determined by a struggle between Capital and Labour from which Nonconformity was organizationally excluded (C.20). Crucially, it might attack the domination of the streets by the young, the hedonistic and the irreverent, but it did not control the flow of migrants, nor the housing market and the size of families which militated against the private pursuit of leisure activities in overcrowded mining districts. Thus, Nonconformity was not the dominant shaping force in Welsh society in this period: it was in fact shaped by the industrialization taking place, which simultaneously and paradoxically enriched the Chapel as it facilitated the growth of often impious alternatives to it in the new migrant communities. That is, Nonconformity might attempt to direct the minds of men, but not the market for miners.

The attempt to direct even the minds of men and women within the Chapel could be undermined by the very independence of the minds being appealed to. One of the unique features of *Dissent* was the power of congregations over their ministers. Ministers were, after all, selected and financially supported by congregations, and *Elders* were elected by them. Always jealous of this control from below, and anxious that it should not be eroded, congregations sought to wield an influence within their domain hitherto not readily attainable outside it. Where that

C.18

C.19

C.20

Evan Roberts and colleague revivalists from Loughor. (*Source: National Library of Wales.*)

control was frustrated there was resistance. Where it was endangered, there was rebellion, often schism.

It is not difficult to find evidence for this process. A purist minister might, by failing to provide for the recreational needs of his flock, provoke a secession of dissidents and the establishment of a new 'cause' more in keeping with their requirements – which often included recourse to the English language (C.21). A congregation embroiled in industrial action, and demanding total solidarity, might indignantly repudiate the calls for reconciliation made by its minister. Always there was simmering resentment at the emerging centralization within the denominations and the accumulation of excessive power over ordinary members and ministers alike by arrogant deacons elected for life (C.22). The Welsh religious revival of 1904–5, usually seen as the final flourish of piety and social conservatism, can also be viewed as another episode in the history of religious self-government in Wales. It was dominated by working-class youth, and by women, and this in a society which offered women almost no paid employment prospects so that

C.21

C.22

82

chapel-going was virtually the only possible and indeed permissible activity outside the family domain. These groups were excluded from a recently professionalized ministry and the *diaconate* by poverty, education, age or gender. Conventionally, the revival has been viewed as encapsulating the crisis of the Nonconformist conscience in an increasingly secular society, as reflecting in some way the guilt of sinners in a fallen world. The analysis presented here allows us to see a different force at work, a force which has rather more to do with democracy than theology. For part of what we see in the explosion of fervour of 1904–5, which by-passed and often despised leaderships, is the frustrations and discontents of the dispossessed (C.23).

C.23

CULTURE

Once we see that linguistic developments can involve questions of power, or that chapel-going can be a form of democratic activity they become difficult to dismiss as of secondary importance. They are as integral to a proper analysis of the whole social process as the economic base. What is at stake in such struggles is the shape of a whole society.

One way of categorizing these activities as a whole is under the heading 'Culture'. Its definition is itself a cause of conflict. Culture is not a list of great books. It is not a 'way of life' which pervades an entire society, from top to bottom. It consists rather of the ways that different, and often opposed, groups of people – the 'rough' and the respectable, men and women, working class and middle class – attempt to assert their humanity and express themselves. As such, culture is a process, a shifting frontier.

To wish to stop this process at one point in time, to isolate a cluster of activities – say the speaking of Welsh or chapel-going – and call them, alone, 'Welsh Culture' is to sacrifice complexity on the altar of myth. And myths are not merely misleading, they are also dangerous: to deny culture to the anglicized or Welshness to the irreligious is after all to exclude majorities from our history. This is why culture matters.

Sources

C.1   I was fascinated by that light in the sky. Night after night I watched it reddening the shadows beyond the *Brecknock Beacon* . . . Tiger noticed my interest in the glare in the sky . . .and he told me 'up there in the works is the place for a young feller. Shorter hours and good money, not like as it be hereabouts – gotter graft all the hours as God sends. Ain't got to call no manner of man sir up there – no yuh ain't' . . . .

    . . . When I hear people extolling the joys of country living I think of the struggles of the small farmers as I knew them. Starting work at five in the morning and leaving off just in time to go to bed about ten at night. . . . No holiday, weekday or sunday, and no other prospect but to get greyer and weaker with the years . . . yet there were others living around us, who were worse off than we were – the farm labourers. They had no right to call a word their own.

    (B. L. Coombes, *These Poor Hands*, 1939, pp.7–12).

C.2   Orchestra in a little something from 'Les Cloches De Cornville' by Offenbach, I think. A gay snatch sung with the orchestra might add to the effect.

Narrator: That, at the very beginning of the not so gay 'Nineties must have been a tonic to the miners who with their wives crowded the sixpenny gallery of the Royal Clarence Theatre nightly. At last a little pleasure, in a real theatre . . . Thanks to it life grew more bearable for miners working a ten hour day . . . Their life had been from bed to work and from work to bed, but *now* there was a little gaiety to be had for sixpence at the Royal Clarence Theatre. Men from the valleys said to their wives 'We'll go even if we have to walk there and back' . . .

Narrator: All this gay music came *after* the opening week, when those who packed the Clarence Theatre nightly were revolted and yet fascinated by Charles Reade's English version of Emile Zola's play, presented under the title of 'Drink'.

(Jack Jones, BBC Broadcast, 1956).

C.3   Mae ysfa troedio'r 'bel ddu' wedi disgyn yn bla ar fechgyn y Deheubarth. Gan dlawd a chyfoethog, crefyddol ac anghrefyddol, y bel droed ydyw pwnc y dydd, a phwnc y nos. Truenus ydyw edrych arnynt bob dydd Sadwrn yn myned gyda'r cerbydresi o'r naill dref i'r llall i gymeryd rhan yn y cystadleuon troedawl. Ac y mae amryw o'r newyddiaduron dyddiol ac wythnosol yn cyflogi gohebwyr i'w dilyn, ac yn hebgor colofnau hirion o'u gofod i roddi adroddiadau manwl o'r campau bwystfilaidd. Onid ydyw pethau fel hyn yn brawf diammheuol fod yr 'oes oleu hon' yn myned yn ei hol i 'dir y tywyllwch'?

(The hankering for kicking the 'black ball' has fallen like plague on the boys of the South. Day and night, for the poor and the wealthy, the religious and the irreligious, football is the talking point . . . And several of the daily and weekly newspapers employ correspondents to cover it, and set aside long columns

Crumlin Football Team, 1900.

for the purpose of giving detailed reports of such bestial sports. Aren't things like this indisputable proof that this 'Age of Light' is returning to the 'Land of Darkness'.)

(*Y Faner*, 4th February, 1885).

C.4   Two parishes, one in Caernarfonshire and one in Merionethshire, were selected by us for detailed examination. In these parishes there were 138 babies under one year of age, and 59 of these were returned as speaking Welsh. There were also 147 infants between one and two years of age, and 87 of these were registered as *monoglot* Welsh. Thus of 285 infants not yet two years of age, 146, or more than a half, were represented as being able to speak Welsh and Welsh only.

Children under two have been excluded by us from the language tables; and, consequently, those strange statements as to their power of speech are not of much importance, excepting that they furnish good grounds for regarding with much suspicion the trustworthiness of the statements as to persons of riper years. Thus in the same two parishes there were 1,587 children of from 5 to 15 years of age, children therefore, who must have had a more or less lengthy period of school attendance. In the schools of both of these parishes English has been taken as a class subject, not without success; yet of these 1,587 children, 1,490, or 94 per cent were returned as unable to speak English . . . We cannot but think that the standard (of proficiency in English) applied must have been unduly high in those parishes.

(1891 *Census, General Report*).

C.5   Tair sir fwyaf Cymraeg y Gogledd yw Meirion Mon ac Arfon – yn y drefn yna. O drigolion y sir, oedd hyn, dros deirblwydd oed, nid oes yn Meirion ond 6 o bob cant yn Saeson uniaith; yn Mon, wyth; ac yn Arfon, deg o bob cant. Ond sylwer: o bob cant o Gymry Meirion, y mae 44 yn gallu siarad y ddwy iaith; 44 hefyd yn Mon; a 42 yn Arfon. Dyma, felly, agos i haner poblogaeth pob un o'r tair sir fwyaf Cymreig yn siarad Cymraeg a Saesneg. Mewn geiriau eraill, dyma'r tair sir ag y mae lleiaf o Saeson yn byw ynddynt eisoes wedi myned yn ddwyieithog.

(The three most Welsh counties of the North are Merioneth, Anglesey and Caernarfon – in that order. Of the inhabitants of those areas over three years old, only 6 per cent in Merioneth, 8 per cent in Anglesey and ten per cent in Caernarvon are English *monoglots*. But note: out of every hundred Merioneth Welsh (Cymry) 44 can speak the two languages; 44 also in Anglesey; and 42 in Caernarfon. The situation therefore is that close to half the population of each of the most Welsh counties speak Welsh and English. In other words the three counties with fewest English inhabitants have already gone bilingual.)

(Revd R. R. Williams, BA, Towyn, referring to the 1901 census in 'Rhwymedigaeth ein Cyfundeb yn ngwyneb Cynnydd yr iaith Saesneg yn ein Gwlad', *Y Goleuad*, 22 December 1901)

C.6   We cannot here discuss in detail all the . . . factors that have contributed to this steady decline of the Welsh language. Welsh nationalists of the more militant type still persist in attributing it to the anti-Welsh policy of the Church, the Imperial Parliament, and to the English system of education in Wales. It has not been due, they say, to any . . . lack of the sentiment of language, among the native population, but to the long-continued and systematic effort of the English and of English officials in Wales, to suppress it in order to crush the spirit of Welsh nationality.

We, however, hold that this view is unhistorical and unjust . . .

In . . . illustration of the unhistorical practice of building up a superstructure of racial and linguistic grievance upon false inferences, we may mention the 'Welsh Note', concerning which so much has been written and spoken, particularly of late years . . . Violent speeches have been made, and acrid articles written, denouncing its tyrannical effect. Its purpose was, we are told, to cause . . . children to look upon the Welsh language as something inferior, even degrading; what invading armies had failed to do, that is, to crush the Welshman's pride in his own country, the English system of education succeeded in doing . . .

But the curious fact is – which Welsh nationalists completely ignore – that the Welsh Note was in vogue during the same period in schools and academies founded and conducted personally by Welsh-speaking Welshmen, some of whom were ministers of religion of the Nonconformist persuasion.

(J. Vyrnwy Morgan, *The Welsh Mind in Evolution*, 1925, pp.129-131).

C.7

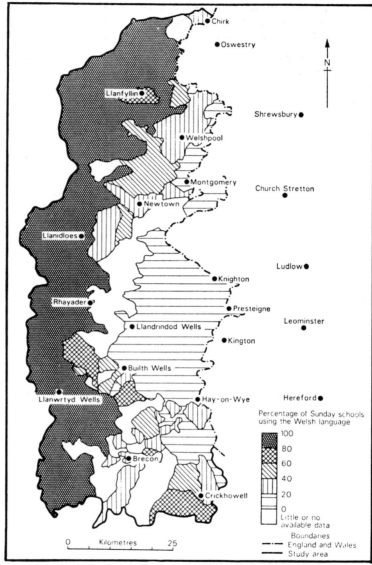

Linguistic areas in the central borderland counties of Wales during the mid-nineteenth century according to the language used at Sunday Schools. (*Source: G. J. Lewis and National Library of Wales. Reproduced from NLW Journal XXI.*)

C.8 . . . ond y Cymry eu hunain sydd yn gollwng y Saesneg i fewn, ac yn gwneud egni i drio y Gymraeg allan o'u teuluoedd, o'u capeli, ac o'u masnach, ac yn llwfr oddef i Saeson ei throi o'n llysoedd cyfreithiol. Mae at ewyllys y Cymry eu hunain i'r Gymraeg farw ne fyw, ac os lleddir hi arnynt hwy eu hunain y bydd y bai. Gofaled pob Cymro gadw ei iaith ar yr aelwyd, yn yr addoldy, ac yn ei fasnach, a hi a fydd bwy.

(. . . it is the Welsh themselves who are letting English in, and making an effort to turn Welsh out of their families, chapels and trade, and timidly allowing the English to turn it out of our law courts. It is up to the Welsh themselves as to whether Welsh dies or lives, and if it dies the blame will be theirs. Let every Welshman keep his language on the hearth, in chapel and in business and it will live.)

(Michael Daniel Jones, *Oes a Gwaith y Prif Athraw y Parch*, Bala, 1903, p.252).

C.9 Ymhen ychydig fisoedd, cafwyd sicrwydd y byddai i'r Bwrdd Addysg dderbyn yr hyn a gymeradwyai'r comisiwn a rhoi'r cwbl mewn grym. Mawr oedd y llawenydd yng nghyfarfod Cymdeithas yr Iaith Gymraeg a gynhaliwyd yn Aberystwyth yn niwedd Mai 1889. A theg yw dweud na chafwyd achos cwyno ar ol hynny oblegid diffyg cydymdeimlad a chefnogaeth ar ran yr awdurdodau yn Llundain. Ni bu neb yn well cyfeillion i'r mudiad na swyddogion addysg yn y brifddinas a'u harolygwyr yng Nghymru.

(Within a few months, it was ascertained that the Education Board would accept what the commission had recommended, and put all of it into force. Great was the joy in the meeting of the *Welsh Language Society* that was held in Aberystwyth at the end of May 1889. And it is fair to say that there was no cause to complain after that of a lack of sympathy and support on the part of the authorities in London. None were better friends to the movement than the Capital's education officials and their inspectors in Wales.)

(John Edward Lloyd, 'Cymdeithas yr Iaith Gymraeg: Trem ar Hanes y Mudiad', *Y Llenor*, 1931, p.209-210).

The managers beg to inform you that not having received application from a single parent to have a child taught Welsh . . . the managers think it unwise to introduce Welsh teaching.

(Secretary to the Managers of Briton Ferry National School, to the Board of Education, 1905. P.R.O. Ed.91/13).

There is far too much apathy in Wales on this subject . . . The time for passing resolutions and bringing pressure to bear upon the Government Department has long since passed. It is the time now for the people and Authorities and Denominations to rouse themselves and do their part on behalf of the mother tongue.

(Alfred Davies, Permanent Secretary to the Welsh Department of the Board of Education. Minute of 6/7/16. P.R.O. Ed.91/57).

. . . the proper quarter to which the efforts of the members of your association as well as of others who share their views, in favour of the teaching of the home language, should be mainly addressed is the local authorities to whom Parliament has entrusted the responsibility for providing education in their respective areas. If local public opinion throughout Wales is fully aroused to the importance of Welsh, the resulting demand for its teaching will undoubtedly make itself felt by the Local Education Authorities and the Governors of Secondary Schools . . . what can be done in the matter by a government department has been and is being done by the *Welsh Department* which cannot be charged with having been slow in showing their realisation of the great value of utilising and fostering the Welsh language to the utmost extent possible. The necessary driving force to enable full advantage to be taken of the facilities offered by the Welsh Department, must however be supplied by people on the spot who are in a position to influence public opinion by the usual methods of the written and spoken word and the vote. You are at liberty to make any use you think fit of this letter which though unofficial may be taken as reflecting the present views and attitude of the Board on the subject.

(Alfred Davies, letter dated 1/7/16. P.R.O. Ed.91/57).

O. M. Edwards. (*Source: Urdd Gobaith Cymru.*)

As to whether the unsatisfactory position occupied by Welsh . . . arises in any and if so, what degree, from any of the following causes:

(a) Want of sympathy or encouragement on the part of the *Board of Education* or its *Welsh Department* or their inspectors;

(b) Lack of enthusiasm for the Welsh language on the part of Local Education Authorities, school managers (elementary) and school governing bodies (secondary);

(c) Failure to make the utmost possible
opportunities given by the *Board of Educ*
regulations, etc, for the teaching or utilisation

Any candid person will be bound to answer '
these questions and 'yes' to the other two . . .

Remind them that it was the *Welsh Department* v
following counsel to the children of Wales which, i.   ⌐u up
by the people of Wales – through whose earnest efforts, not
through the recommendations of any Departmental Committee
of Government Department will Welsh be kept alive as the
language of hearth and home, the places where it flourishes best
as a living tongue:

Question 'How can Welsh children uphold the Welsh
Language?'

Answer 'By speaking, by reading and by writing it whenever
they can – at home or abroad, at work or at play. A good
knowledge of Welsh is a thing to be proud of, and all Welsh
children should praise their mother tongue accordingly'.

(Welsh Department of the Board of Education, St David's Day
pamphlet, 1915)

Responsibility for maintaining and strengthening the position
and improving the teaching of the Welsh language must not be
allowed to be shifted from Whitehall to the Principality.

It is fairly certain that no government department within the
British Empire, or indeed any central government, has ever
given such warm encouragement to the use of the mother
tongue as is to be found in the foregoing and other like advice
which has issued during the last 16 years from the *Welsh
Department*.

Possibly what is now needed in the way of a stimulant is a
little hostility and less benevolence towards the native language
on the part of the central authority! Though I should be sorry to
prescribe that as a remedy for a condition of things which
admittedly is certainly not satisfactory.

(Sir Alfred T. Davies, Permanent Secretary to the Welsh
Department of the Board of Education, in a memo to the
President 17th January, 1923, re. the questions to be asked of

visiting deputation of Central Welsh Board and Court of University of Wales. P.R.O. Ed.91/57).

C.10   3. LANGUAGE   THE LINGUISTIC CONDITIONS OF THE SIX COUNTIES IN WALES WHICH CONTAIN ANY CONSIDERABLE INDUSTRIAL POPULATION IS ALSO SHOWN IN THE FOLLOWING TABLE:

TABLE F — LANGUAGE SPOKEN, 1911

County	Monoglot Welsh	Monoglot English	Bilinguals	Unknown or Foreign
	Percentage	*Percentage*	*Percentage*	*Percentage*
Brecknock	5.45	57.1	36	1.45
Carmarthen	20.5	13.35	64.5	1.65
Denbigh	10.05	41.66	46.62	1.67
Flint	3.5	55.35	38.75	2.4
Glamorgan	3.07	58.00	35.03	3
Monmouth	0.41	86.27	9.25	4.07

(*Commission of Inquiry into Industrial Unrest, No.7 Div. Report of the Commissioners for Wales, including Monmouthshire* (1917)).

C.11   The Welsh were in a minority in Tai-Harry-Blawd, where they were mixed with English, Irish and Scotch people, whose fathers and grandfathers had been brought into Wales by the old Iron Kings. At first I knew only Welsh from my parents and grandparents, but as I went on playing with the Scott, Hartley, Ward and McGill children, I became more fluent than in my native language. Dad was annoyed when I started replying in English to what he had said in Welsh, but our mam said, in Welsh: 'Oh, let him alone. What odds, anyway?'

(Jack Jones, *Unfinished Journey*, London, 1938, p.22).

C.12   Sir, A good number of our Welsh parents cannot prevail upon their own children to learn the Welsh language upon their own hearths and among their own family and I admit that it is a most difficult matter in many instances in a town like Pontypridd where the English tongue is so predominant among all classes. Even in the Welsh chapel after a Welsh service we find as soon as the service is over that most of the conversation takes place in English.

(Letter from 'Non Con', *Glamorgan Free Press*, 26 April, 1902)

C.13   We understand that the *Independents* of Rhydfelen visited Mr
Hamlen Williams at Fairfield. While the participants were
indulging in various games in the field they were rudely assailed
by a banded squad of Pontypridd 'uncontrollables' who
marched about interrupting the past-times, much to the
annoyance of all. They would not enjoy themselves neither
would they allow others to do so. When civilly reprimanded
by a ministerial gentleman their harsh retorts were most
degrading. One of the 'squad' especially replied most rudely to
his civil injunctions, and out of sheer disrespect and ignorance,
sarcastically commenced to sing a Welsh hymn in which the
whole 'squad' participated. The ministerial gentleman turned
away in disgust. It is to be regretted that such scandalous
behaviour is permitted. We hope that the approaching demonstration at Pontypridd will not be invaded by such a 'set'.

(*Glamorgan Free Press*, 8 July, 1893).

The population comprises a very rough one. The local police
often experience great difficulties there in quelling disturbances
and more particularly in arresting and conveying prisoners to
Pontypridd. The rougher populace taking the advantage of
there being no lock-up station in their midst.
(Jabez Matthews, Deputy Chief Constable in Return of population, licensed hours, public works and particulars where a
county lock-up police station at Ynysybwl is found to be
necessary for the preservation of the peace, 1890. GRO D/D
Con).

C.14   Ystariaf fy hun yn Gymro gwladgarol iawn; ond, ar yr un pryd,
nid oes gennyf ond achos i barchu y cenhedloedd sydd yn yr un
ymherodraeth a ni. Beth bynnag fu'r Sais yn yr hen amser,
ystyriaf mai'r Prydeiniwr yw cyfaill gonestai rhyddid heddyw.
Y mae'r Almaen yn alltudio hyd yn oed merched gweini o'r
rhannau Danaidd am siarad iaith eu tadau: ac y mae Rwsia
othrymus newydd gyhoeddi fod yn rhaid i bob swyddog drwy
Finland fedru siarad Rwsiaeg. Ond gellir siarad Cymraeg
trwy holl gynghorau Cymru. Waeth heb grochfloeddio
gwladgarwch ar ddygwyl Dewi tra y mae Cymry yn gwrthod
siarad Cymraeg yn eu cynghorau lleol eu hunain.

(I consider myself a very patriotic Welshman; but at the same time I have nothing but cause to respect the nations in the same empire as us. Whatever the Englishman was in the past, I consider the Briton to be the most honest friend of freedom today. Germany exiles even serving girls from the Danish parts for speaking the language of their fathers; and oppressive Russia has just announced that every official in Finland must be able to speak Russian. But Welsh can be spoken in all the councils in Wales. It would be best to forgo declaiming patriotism on St David's Day whilst Welsh people refuse to speak Welsh in their own local councils . . . The government is not to blame now; we are.)

(O. M. Edwards replying to a correspondent in *Cymru* Vol.16, 1899, p.148).

C.15   Welsh . . . is the medium through which the mass of the people can receive intellectual culture and give expression to their own genius. You will therefore we hope be inclined to agree with us that the language ought to be systematically taught in order that it may be the salutary factor that it ought to be in the national life.

(Alfred Thomas, MP to the Secretary for Education, A. Birrell, 1906, PRO Ed.91/13).

C.16   (a) Welsh. Though a large proportion of the parents knew Welsh, it seems very clear that many of them neglect to speak it in the home, and that the children therefore have little opportunity to hear or speak the language. It is to be feared that the want of enthusiasm on the part of some teachers, finds some apparent justification in this apathy of the parents. Steps should be taken to awaken the public to a sense of the loss sustained by this attitude.

(General Report of Her Majesty's Inspectors on Elementary Education in the Urban District of Pontypridd for the Period ending July 31, 1913, (Original Manuscript: unpublished) PRO Ed.91/35).

(b) Welsh – A large proportion of the parents of the district know Welsh; and, in speaking Welsh to their children at home, they take an important part in the education of their children. The home and the school will provide for the teaching of Welsh, the street and the school for the teaching of English.

(*General Report of Her Majesty's Inspectors on Elementary Education in the Urban District of Pontypridd for the Period ending July 31, 1913*, (published version of the above), PRO Ed.91/35).

C.17 Congregations will be regarded as the conservators of effete superstitions if they do not step out from the formalism of their round of services into the midst of the struggling, starving, sorrowing, sinning world around them.

(*North Wales Congregational Magazine*, September 1891).

Were churches what they professed to be why should their young men seek their pleasures in play-houses and on football fields? Football he declared to be the dullest and most senseless game the world had ever seen (Laughter). Even an ape . . . would not disgrace itself by seeking its pleasures in kicking a football. Why, if they and middle aged men found any pleasure in going to the pubs, theatres and football field, then let them, in the name of God and for the honour, success and influence of the Church upon the world remain outside her pale (Applause).

(Revd John Rees, *South Wales Daily News*, 5 May, 1894).

C.18 How would these very good people like to live days, weeks, months underground without a sight of the sun, and then on a wet Sunday to keep within doors all the sunless hours, except while attending divine worship? Oh, these very generous people have their nice cosy clubs or homes which they enjoy every day. But the collier has to live in discomfort in a small home, and for near six months in every year never sees the sun except on the first day of the week.

(*Merthyr Express*, 30 July, 1881, letter from a workman).

EMPIRE,

Theatre of Varieties, TONYPANDY.

Proprietors - **THE TONYPANDY THEATRE OF VARIETIES, LTD.**
Resident Manager - - - **Mr. S. M. B. HOOLE.**

GRAND OPENING
Monday, November 15th, 1909.

✂ PROGRAMME. ✂
NATIONAL ANTHEM

1 SELECTION .. .. By the Orchestra

2 MARGARET MONKS .. .. Dainty Singer of Chorus Songs

3 HARRY FRISKEY As "THE DINING ROOM INTRUDER."
The Unique American Comedy Juggler.

4 ROBB WILTON .. .. The Confiding Comedian

5 BEATRICE ENGLISH .. .. .. World's Premier Vocalist

6 WOOD WELKINS & CO. In a Vocal Comedy Sketch, "THE PIANO
TUNER."

7 B. A. ROLFE'S production of **"YE COLONIAL SEPTETTE"**
Presenting "AN OLDE TYME HALLOWE'EN," featuring
Mr. CHARLES EDWARDS, America's Cornet Virtuoso

    Scene 1 ... ... **The Prologue**
    Scene 2 ... **The Gate in the garden wall**
    Scene 3 **Drawing Room of a Colonial Mansion**

CAST

Mr. WILLIAM GALPEN   Basso
Mr. RAYMOND EVANS   Trombonist
Miss NETTIE COBURN   Cornetist
Miss FLORA GARRIS   Violinist

Prologue spoken by Miss LILIAN GARRIS.
Witches Horn played by Mr. CHARLES HARRIS.
and
Mr. Charles Edwards   **The American Cornet Virtuoso**

8 L. J. SEYMOUR Character and Actor Vocalist, in his Great and
Latest Racing Episode, "ONLY A JOCKEY," or "DERBY
DAY."

9 LE ROUX'S CYCLING MONKEYS .. The Most Marvellous
Example of Animal Training Extant

10 EMPIROSCOPE .. .. .. Entertaining and Interesting

GOD SAVE THE KING.

Souvenir programme, printed on silk, for the first performance at the Empire Theatre of Varieties, Tonypandy, 15 November 1909. (*Source: Cyril Batstone.*)

C.19 Our columns week by week unfold a social state which is not flattering to the influence of educational and religious agencies in the town of Pontypridd. The prostitution which is open and almost defiant in our midst and which is even over-matching the best and most vigilant attention of the police must be persistently attacked by the authorities if the putrid contagion is to be arrested in its baneful career of blight and disrepute to the name of the town.

(*Glamorgan Free Press*, 4 January, 1894).

C.20 There is talk that the colliers' monthly holiday is becoming a nuisance. Taking last Monday for instance, the natural conclusion is that but few comparatively spend the day in a rational manner. Hundreds are to be found in a state of drunkenness during the day. Surely this was not the way in which it was intended that the monthly holiday should be spent.

There is considerable difference of opinion as to whether the holiday is a boon or a bane. The calendic day off is doubtless intended to be of 'mutual benefit' to the coal-digging community of the Rhondda but it is very much doubted whether the intention is observed or even recognised by the large majority of the colliers . . . the sooner the abolition of the holiday is brought about the better.

Complaints have for some time been roused amongst leaders of the workmen that the day fixed by them for meetings to discuss their own welfare has been seized upon by publicans and all sorts of clever financiers for the purpose of money-making. There were certainly many counter-attractions provided last Monday which drew a larger number of people from the Hafod than attended the great mass meeting held in Bethel Chapel, notwithstanding the presence of three MPs. Flowers of rhetoric and flights of oratory are all very well in their way, but when counter-balanced by such attractions as a glove fight, two races and a *coursing match* or two, what can be expected?

(*Pontypridd Chronicle*, 5 April, 7 June, 8 November, 1899).

C.21 To show the tendency of the desire for English in this town, even among Welsh-speaking parents, practically all the Welsh

Sunday Schools have introduced English teaching. A very striking instance of the preference given to English is the case of a Welsh congregation in this parish. Through dissension in the congregation they have had what is called in Wales a 'split' i.e. a number of the congregation leaving the mother chapel and building one for themselves. The divided congregations have just had their annual Sunday School Tea, when the mother chapel (Welsh) numbered 180, and the 'split' party, who adopted English in their form of worship, numbered 220.

(Secretary of the Managers of Briton Ferry National School to the Board of Education, 27 July, 1905. PRO Ed.91/13).

C.22   Tredegar has been thrown into a state of excitement by a chapel split, the climax of which was reached last Sunday, when the minister and congregation, proceeding to the morning service, found themselves unable to gain admission, the gate and the doors being locked. The unfortunate rupture has taken place at Oakfield Road Congregational Church . . .

For some time it has been whispered that there has been friction among the members, who are apparently divided into two sections, one of whom are supporters of Alderman Henry Bowen, the senior deacon, and the other of the pastor, the Reverend C. E. Morgan. At the outset the points of difference were of a somewhat unimportant nature, but the recent election of deacons aggravated them to a serious extent. Exception was taken by Alderman Bowen and his followers to the method of election and on Sunday night week at the chapel meeting, opinions were emphatically exchanged upon it. Another meeting on Thursday evening did not tend to heal the difference and then on Sunday morning, the closing of the chapel brought the matter to a crisis. Upon making inquiries, the pastor found that instructions had been given not to deliver up the keys to him or any of his followers. Undismayed, services were held in the open air upon a space adjacent to the chapel, which remained closed all day.

Seen by our Tredegar reporter, Alderman Bowen stated that the rupture had reached such an acute stage that he kept the place locked because he was afraid of serious disturbances between rival factions. He still maintained that the recent election of deacons took place on unconstitutional lines. His action was taken on the authority of being sole trustee of the chapel.

The pastor, the Revd C. E. Morgan, on the other hand, maintains that the election was perfectly legal. The vote was by ballot, and the new deacons were afterwards adopted practically unanimously by the Chapel. The reverend gentleman said he had the majority of members with him, and added that services would be held in temporary premises for the time being. The pastor complained bitterly of the action of Alderman Bowen, which he characterised as high-handed and unjustified, and indicated that legal opinion was being taken as to his procedure.

(*South Wales Weekly Argus*, 18 September, 1909).

C.23   A Cwmavon minister who had not been allowed to preach for several Sundays approached a group of young men between the ages of 16 and 23: 'Am I to preach tonight' . . . 'It depends upon what the Spirit tells us' . . . The pastor as a representative of the normal type of religious experience was practically regarded as an alien in the Commonwealth of Israel. The prevailing sentiment was expressed in the prayer of the man who thanked the Lord that He had shunted the ministers on the side line . . .

The same unsympathetic attitude was assumed by *Evan Roberts* towards aged Christians. In his presence young men deprecated the restraining influence of the old and actually prayed for their conversion and in some instances even for their removal by death This side of the Revival was not noticed in the press reports The insolence the young men were encouraged to cultivate towards the aged may be classed as one of the saddest features of the Revival of 1904–5.

(J. Vyrnwy Morgan, *The Welsh Religious Revival 1904–5: A Retrospect and Criticism*, 1909, pp.42, 184, 189).

Debating the Evidence

The range of documents at the disposal of the historian continues to widen with this selection. There is one familiar source – a census report, although it is instructive to compare this extract with the census material which John Williams provides in Section A. Less familiar kinds of sources include autobiography, a transcript of a radio broadcast and a variety of commentaries from newspapers and books. A feature of these is that they are not engaged in factual reporting but for the most part in analysis, more or less profound, of the emotive subject of the state of the Welsh language. We need to be very conscious here of the unwitting testimony, or unintentional record, of this material. It testifies to considerable apprehension throughout the century over the fate of the Welsh language. The witting testimony is far more difficult to interpret since virtually all this evidence is opinion, not record.

Source C.1

What information would you need to have about B. L. Coombes before using this source?

Source C.3

Y Faner was (and still is) a Welsh-language journal. Does this information help in evaluating the worth of this source? What further information would you now require?

Source C.4

Do you agree with the arguments propounded here?

Source C.5

How far is this a neutral statement of the state of the Welsh language in north-west Wales?

Source C.6

What does this extract tell you about J. Vyrnwy Morgan?

Source C.7

Try putting the information conveyed in this diagram into words. What vital piece of information is missing in the reference provided here?

Source C.8

What information would you like to have about Michael D. Jones before using this document?

Source C.9

How might you set about confirming J. E. Lloyd's generalizations? Lloyd was a professor of history in the University of Wales and author of one of the great histories of Wales. How might this influence you in assessing this extract? How well does Lloyd's statement square with the other C.9 documents?

Source C.10

How reliable do you think would the statistical evidence be from a Commission of Enquiry?

Sources C.12 and C.13

Do you regard these as useful historical evidence? It would be useful, as always, to distinguish between the intentional and unintentional record.

Sources C.14, C.15 and C.16

What do these documents tell you about the people who wrote them?

Sources C.17 (both) and C.18

What information would you require about the authors and the newspapers before deciding on the reliability of this evidence?

Source C.22

What does this extract tell us about (a) Tredegar (b) *The South Wales Weekly Argus* (c) the readership of *The South Wales Weekly Argus*, in 1909?

Discussion

There is one particularly significant source provided here – Source C.7. It is interesting because it is a secondary source in one sense. We are not provided with its date of publication (this is the information missing from Source C.7) but it certainly came into existence long after the period which we are studying. It is built up from primary sources, particularly statistics of Sunday schools and their language. This information could well have been analysed in a written paragraph but the author has chosen to 'translate' this information into diagrammatic form. Its impact is immediate and its message much more direct than if he had merely described his findings. Here is a salutary reminder of how maps and other diagrammatic and pictorial representation are such a valuable tool for the historian.

Much of the rest of this source section is taken from autobiographies and newspapers. The dangers of autobiographical evidence are obvious. Memory might be genuinely at fault. The author may be purposely selective so as to demonstrate, if not always good judgement, at least the best motives for bad judgement. Such historical record has to be treated with great caution, yet it is invaluable. It provides essential information about attitudes, often formed by first-hand acquaintance with the events under discussion.

Newspaper and journal evidence is crucial to the historian of more recent periods. Local newspapers, particularly, provide an invaluable record of events which may only assume significance in retrospect, as well as recording major happenings. More than this, they provide a forum for a wide variety of opinion, through editorials, reporters' comments and letters columns. The nineteenth century was the golden age of journals and periodicals in Welsh. Each religious denomination, for example, had its journal and through it provided not only a forum for theological debate but for political and social discussion of the sort we see represented here. Newspapers and journals need, also, to be treated with particular care. We are all aware that even so-called factual reporting in the press is not always well-informed. There was a recent article in *The Guardian* about the British Steel Industry which claimed that one of the Port Talbot plant's advantages was that it was *close* to facilities at Shotton. One wonders how much of the rest of the article to take seriously. When we come to editorials, comments and correspondence, there are many more question marks. Who owned the paper? Did the owner(s) consistently pursue a particular party line or did they not interfere in editorial matters? What was the editor's political stance, in terms of national and local politics? What were his views on religion and language in Wales during this period? Who were the reporters involved and what were their attitudes? Of course, it may not always be possible to find this information, particularly in the case of individual reporters, but it is possible to get the flavour of the line taken by any newspaper if we sample its contents regularly.

Again, these documents raise the matter of witting and unwitting testimony (intentional and unintentional record) as being of particular significance. In sources such as those cited here, there is invaluable evidence of widespread concern in the period after 1880 about the fate of the Welsh language. It is also obvious that the debate over who was responsible had also been opened up early on. This is interesting because the 1901 census revealed that, while in percentage terms the situation was serious – just under 50 per cent could now speak Welsh, in terms of absolute numbers more people could speak the language than ever. But there is no mistaking the sense of foreboding. As to responsibility for what was going on, the evidence which Tim Williams provides here seems to indicate unequivocally that Government bodies were anything but hostile to the language. Yet it remains that, at least since the 1880s, there has been a popular view in Wales that the English Government and educational institutions have viewed the prospect of the disappearance of the language with equanimity. This is a most potent myth which prevails still. It is in contradiction to the testimony of the evidence here.

Price—ONE PENNY.

THE

MINERS' NEXT STEP

BEING A SUGGESTED SCHEME FOR THE

Reorganisation of the Federation

Issued by the Unofficial Reform Committee

TONYPANDY :

ROBERT DAVIES AND CO., GENERAL PRINTERS, ETC.

1912.

Title page of *The Miners' Next Step*. (*Source: South Wales Miners' Library.*)

From Riots to Revolt: Tonypandy and The Miners' Next Step

DAVID SMITH

In recent years historians have drastically revised their interpretation of those pre-1914 industrial troubles which go under
the name of The Great Labour Unrest. There were, it is true,
serious disturbances and bitter strikes in 1910, in 1911 and 1913,
in places as remote from each other as Tonypandy and Dublin,
as near as Llanelli and Tredegar, as connected in trade as
Liverpool and Cardiff. Two men were indeed shot down by
troops in the rail strike at Llanelli in 1911 and troops had killed
two others on the streets of Liverpool in that city's general
transport strike in the same year. The strikes often spilled over
into a more general attack on property and property owners
who had no direct connection with the disputes. Social revolt
seemed to go hand in hand with industrial militancy to such an
extent that some feared, and others hoped for, revolutionary
upsurge, based on direct action by trade unions and bypassing
parliamentary socialism, that would actually confront the state
itself in a General Strike for all workers. The subsequent
victory, prepared for by successful strikes in particular industries, would ushers in workers' control of the production
and distribution of all goods, industry by industry, for the
benefit of all rather than the profit of a few. This doctrine was
widely proclaimed and its supporters known as 'syndicalists'
(after the French 'Syndic' or union) or 'industrial unionists'
(since they wanted all workers in any one type of industry to be
organized in one big union).

On the other hand, the fury of the revolts, impelled by falling
wages in a climate of relatively high employment, had died away
by 1913. The more moderate, conciliatory union leaders had not

been removed in influence nor, with some exceptions, in person. The leadership of the Parliamentary Labour Party had always been firmly anti-syndicalist and argued for a long-term strategy of winning a parliamentary majority and then implementing policies of state nationalization of key industries. In 1912 this is precisely what the *MFGB* (Miners' Federation of Great Britain) put forward as its aim. When this was finally delivered in 1947 by the 1945 Labour government the debate seemed finally over: after all syndicalism had had nothing to show for its early optimism other than the great strikes of 1919 to 1921 and the failure of the 1926 General Strike. The number of workers organized in trade unions (rising dramatically from 1910 on) plummeted again after 1926, and only climbed slowly back towards the end of the 1930s.

In this broad context, then, the name 'Tonypandy' and the 1912 pamphlet published there (*The Miners' Next Step*) are little more than minor footnotes. The riots of 1910 and the local syndicalism of 1912 can both be explained, within a British pattern of social and economic change, as interesting aberrations of behaviour. Certainly it is true that there is no difficulty in describing accurately the events of 1910–11 in mid-Rhondda which are known as the Cambrian Combine Strike. The Combine had been welded together in 1908 from existing colliery companies by *D. A. Thomas*, coalowner and Liberal MP. Under the general management of Leonard Llewellyn it produced 50 per cent of the Rhondda's coal output and maximised profits by advanced cost-efficiency methods. In its employ were over 12,000 men. Throughout 1909 negotiations were underway to settle a new cutting price for a seam in the Ely pit. When no agreement could be reached the management locked out all 800 Ely workmen on 1st September 1910. The Cambrian Combine employees in the other pits in the environs of the township of Tonypandy saw this as the first move in a plan to undercut their piece-rate wages too (i.e. the amount they received per ton of coal cut) and, from 1st November, all the pits stopped work. Despite a lack of enthusiastic support by the official *SWMF* (South Wales Miners' Federation) leadership the men stayed out until the high summer of 1911 when they returned on the wages and conditions they were offered in

October 1910. It was a bitter pill to swallow. Even so the issue of a minimum wage and the allied fair treatment for men working underground in 'abnormal places' (i.e. where water, or the height of the roof, or, as in the case of the Ely pit, the amount of stone in the coal made much work unproductive or 'dead') would not go away. In 1912 the British miners struck for, and won, at least some provision for a minimum wage.

Historians who have puzzled over the persistence of 'Tonypandy' as legend and myth in the history of the Labour movement have been driven to re-examine the story by discarding the hindsight which has shaped our sense of 'Tonypandy' as part of an unfolding series of events. From this perspective the shock 'Tonypandy' administered to contemporaries, the longevity of its wider influence and the significance of the attached syndicalist doctrines became clear again. In some ways it is the sources themselves which blurred our vision and it is only through re-interpretation and comparison of different types of source material that the focus can be sharpened.

At first sight the most difficult problem to resolve is the contentious issue that centres around *Winston Churchill* and the troop movements of 1910. To what extent was he responsible for the presence of the military in mid-Rhondda, and what effect did this have on events (D.1)? The clarity of the questions has not been generally reflected in the answers given. As late as 1978 there were scenes of uproar in the House of Commons when, in reply to a routine question on miners' pay by *Churchill*'s grandson, another Winston Churchill MP, the Labour Prime Minister, James Callaghan, accused the Churchill family of pursuing a vendetta against miners and threw in the name of 'Tonypandy' for good measure. He refused to withdraw and claimed that, at the very least, *Churchill*'s actions were a matter of historical dispute. That was true. But it scarcely needed to be since the evidence, though complex, is clear enough.

As early as 2 November 1910, authorities in south Wales were enquiring about the procedure for requesting military aid in the event of disturbances because of the strike (in addition to the Cambrian Combine dispute there was a month-old strike in the neighbouring Cynon Valley) and in the Rhondda the Chief

D.1

Tonypandy, early twentieth century. (*Sources: Welsh Industrial and Maritime Museum* and *Cyril Batstone*.)

Constable of Glamorgan had, by Sunday 6 November, concentrated over 200 imported police in the area. It was this force he judged inadequate after the attack on the Glamorgan colliery on 7 November. His request for troops went straight to the War Office and, immediately, troops were entrained.

Churchill, as Home Secretary, now learned of this movement
D.2 (D.2) and, after a brief conference with the War Office halted it. He rightly surmised that the local authorities were over-reacting and certainly hoped that a Liberal government could calm matters down. However, he did accede to the extent of despatching *Metropolitan police* officers (foot and mounted) and
D.3 some troops (the cavalry) did proceed to Cardiff that day (D.3). *Churchill's* personal message to the strikers was to the effect that 'We are holding back the soldiers for the present and sending only police'. This could be seen as a veiled threat more than a promise. In any case, after telephone conversations later that day and even before the *Stipendiary Magistrate's* 7.45 telegram
D.4 (D.4), the Home Office did agree to authorize military support
D.5 (D.5). This occurred *after* the further clashes outside the Glamorgan colliery but *before* Tonypandy itself was, in the words of reporter David Evans, 'sacked'.

D.6 All of this, and the subsequent stationing of troops (D.6), is plainly recorded in the Home Office's published volume of 1911 entitled *Colliery Strike Disturbances in South Wales: Correspondence and Report 1910* from which Sources D.2–6, D.8 and D.19 are taken. Furthermore the troops were stationed in the area until the strike was virtually ended in 1911.

It could be argued that *Churchill* was, in the context of his times, doing no less than his duty as a Home Secretary. Indeed, his *Tory* opponents did suggest that he should have acted with greater vigour. There is no doubt, either, that the troops acted more circumspectly and were commanded with greater common sense than the police forces whose role under the peppery Lionel Lindsay was indeed that of an army of occupation. The troops were not regarded by the community with the same level of hostility as were the police.

So why did this incident continue to haunt *Churchill* throughout his political career? David Evans's 1911 account gives one reason why. The troops did *not* remain 'in the

D.1   background', as *Churchill* claimed in 1950 (D.1), for their
        essential role was to allow the police to control all demonstra-
        tions against '*blackleg*' (or strike-breaking) labour. On more
        than one occasion the troops went further and came into direct
D.7   contact with the strikers (D.7). The troops ensured that trials of
        rioters, strikers and trade union leaders would take place and
        be successfully prosecuted in 1911 in Pontypridd. Straight-
        forwardly, their presence prevented the mass picketing that
        might have ended the strike early in the strikers' favour. In
        addition, *Churchill* had, in any case, added to the police brought
        in by Lindsay so that well over 1,000 were billeted in mid-
        Rhondda. The defeat of 1911 was, in the eyes of the local
        community, attached directly to state intervention without any
        negotiation.

        This was not forgotten when *Churchill*, now a bellicose
        Conservative minister in *Stanley Baldwin*'s 1926 cabinet, actively
        encouraged rapid troop movements during the General Strike.
        In 1940, as *Chamberlain*'s war-time government faltered and
        Churchill was poised to be his successor, *Clement Attlee* (Leader
        of the Labour Party) secretly warned that the Labour Party
        might not follow *Churchill* into a coalition government because
        of the association of his name with that of Tonypandy. Thus his
        unexpected, and unprovoked, reference to Tonypandy in 1950
        was not without point if he could persuade his listeners that his
D.8   motives had been as liberal as they were sensible (D.8). Only it
        was not motives he chose to defend, but rather deeds which
        were recalled forty years on with more panache than accuracy.

        If it is the connection of a great man with small, half-
        forgotten facts which has unnecessarily bedevilled the
        historiography of the Tonypandy riots, the events of the night
        of Tuesday 8 November after the clash with the police outside
        the Glamorgan colliery in Llwynypia were genuinely be-
        wildering. Undoubtedly, the commercial high street of nearby
        Tonyandy was wrecked. But why? What motives underlay this
        violent behaviour?

        After it was over many observers, including leading socialists
        like *Keir Hardie*, MP for Merthyr since 1900, argued that it was
        the work of a small group of people, many of them drunk, and
        that it was inaugurated by police brutality. The level of violence

was consistently played down or condemned outright by the local union leaders. And yet newspaper accounts, a list of the damage (60 shops seriously smashed) and eyewitnesses' recollections leave us in no doubt that thousands of men, women and children were involved in riotous behaviour that lasted for hours. And the public houses had been closed early that day.

David Evans had more clear-cut answers. He wrote his lively, if lurid, account on behalf of his employers, the coalowners, to vindicate their case and to justify the activities of the police. In part his narrative is designed to refute the military commander's, General Macready's, cooler view of events by stressing the real danger to property and the necessary heroism of the police in its defence. According to Evans the 'mob', having prevented any working at the other Cambrian Combine collieries on 7 November, decided to storm the Glamorgan colliery where police and officials had been marshalled inside the Power House to keep pumps and fans going in the pit. Foiled in their endeavours by fierce police resistance they

D.9   wreaked cowardly revenge on the shopkeepers (D.9). This is the motivation most people accepted. *Churchill* offered it to King George V as sole explanation. This was the 'anarchy' that incensed the outside world and over which local union leaders and socialists shook their heads gravely. But the fact of the matter is, as oral evidence and contemporary newspaper accounts make clear, that the crowd never intended to seize the Power House. Throughout the dispute they were determined to stop any working by officials, imported labour or any other '*blacklegs*' and to halt the collieries even at the risk of flooding. They stoned the Power house in a crowd of around 9,000 on 8 November but they did not take the Power House even though they beat back the police who had charged *them* in an effort to disperse the demonstration. General Macready dispassionately establishes the ease with which the crowd could have captured

D.10   the colliery if that had been their aim (D.10). They were certainly bloodied and battered by police charges but, as

D.11   PC Knipe remembered, scarcely beaten into submission (D.11).

We require, then, another explanation for the riot against the town. Crowd actions in pre-industrial societies have been investigated with considerable sophistication in the last thirty years by historians determined to re-establish the human, concrete detail hidden by such value-loaded abstractions as 'the mob' or 'the masses'. Industrial crowd action, on the other hand, has more readily been linked to the strike activity that usually surrounds it in a cause-and-effect manner. This is perhaps, too convenient. Tonypandy, along with much of south Wales in 1910, was a society-in-the-making. Often raw and raucous, basic in amenities, base in some of its pleasures, afflicted by appalling rates of infant and maternal mortality, occasionally shattered by the devastating effect of mass death in pit explosions and continually renewed by a spectacular rising population, the mid-Rhondda was a community in the process of defining its identity. The social elite of the township of Tonypandy was, above all others, the shop-owning class. The angry, wealth-producing crowd turned against the symbol of social attainment, the conspicuous, wealth-making shops. And they did so in a manner that expressed contempt and resentment rather than greed and fear.

D.12

D.13

The shops were smashed systematically but not indiscriminately (D.12). The amount of looting was not so important as the display of bravado enacted on the streets. Goods were scattered about on the road. Clothes were worn in parade – top hats and overcoats in a festival atmosphere – and mufflers, braces and caps (more useful items to colliers) pinched and exchanged as trophies (D.13). Women and children were involved in considerable numbers, as they had been outside the Glamorgan colliery. No police were seen until the *Metropolitans* arrived around 10.30pm (almost 3 hours after the riots began) and then the disturbance fell away of its own accord. Some shops were completely untouched – the most famous exception to the general damage done to chemists' establishments being that of Willie Llewellyn who had the good luck to be known as Wales's greatest wing-threequarter of the day!

The violence was, of course, unplanned and (sometimes) without a specific direction for its rage. Nonetheless the way in which the crowd acted in avoiding some targets and the obvious way in which it was more concerned with overt destruction and display than covert pillage and concealment is a real clue to the significance of the riot. This general move against the public side of a community proud of its progressive, dynamic society yet less concerned about the greater realities of lives that were nasty, brutish and short, is our indication of how sure the crowd was that the shopkeeping class *should* be formally, if rather unceremoniously, involved directly in an industrial dispute that was about the *whole* nature of this mining community.

Besides, historical enquiry that does not attempt to explain the riot in terms of the whole process of community development is like conducting a murder investigation according to the rules of *Cluedo*. If we look at either side of the events of 7–8 November we can discover the constant anxiety of shopkeepers

D.14 about the loss of profits a prolonged strike would entail (D.14), their very close involvement and expressed admiration for the local coalowners and mine managers and their private, often secret, deliberations on credit facilities and police protection. Newspaper stories and Chamber of Trade minutes, as well as editorials and correspondence columns, fill out a picture of a community frequently shaped and cajoled by its shopkeeping

D.15 elite. They were at the centre of the public stage (D.15). Advertisements remind us of their urgent appeals for colliers' wives' custom and photographs of the bustle and pretension of their public world. Even more to the point than any of this surmise (for historical reconstruction of crowd behaviour is, too, imaginative guess-work) is the clinching evidence we have of the crucial role played by shopkeepers in the domestic arrangements of their clients. Houses, to own and to rent, were in short supply. Speculative building was a profitable exercise. Shopkeepers possessed the capital and the local interest to

D.16 become multi-house-owners (D.16). Undoubtedly, some of them took a further advantage of this state of affairs by charging exorbitant or unfairly assessed rents, by making tenants shop in their stores, by positively encouraging overcrowding in order to have large families dependent on them for foodstuffs or furniture and even renting rooms to the highest bidder. All of this was complained about in the Rhondda, especially by the Trades and Labour Council, for up to *five* years before the Tonypandy riots and it was officially confirmed in a sensational

D.17 report by the Medical Officer of Health in 1911 (D.17). Anger may have sparked off the crowd's attack on 8 November 1910,

Tonypandy after the riots. (*Sources: Cyril Batstone;* and *Welsh Industrial and Maritime Museum.*)

but a deep, local knowledge directed their action.

However, the riot against commercial property, even more than the attacks on the collieries, was clearly outside any accepted sense of normality. If the action taken was not that of an incensed mob it must surely have been directed by leaders. This was the opinion of General Macready who came to know the articulate leaders of the strikers and rapidly decided some of them were determined to create a new, 'socialist' society (D.18). There is little to be said for this argument insofar as it relates to the riots directly. To begin with, the local strike committee, and the leaders imprisoned for incitement to riot against *blacklegs* in 1911, were neither firebrands nor 'syndicalists'. They could excuse, but they did not condone, the attacks on shopkeepers. Those who were convinced of the necessity of socialist politics (and not all were) concluded that the social and industrial disruption was a sign of working-class disquiet that had political potential *if* it was channelled away from momentary acts of violence. What was needed was not justification of the outburst but the direction of energies so expressed into effective industrial and political organizations. Now, since the mid-Rhondda did, in retrospect, contain such a 'small but energetic section' preaching 'the doctrine of extreme socialism' the ideological framework of syndicalism/socialism has become a surround for the causes of the strike and its bitter course. And yet, apart from the very real connection of certain men and their later careers with the immediate events in Tonypandy, the strike and the riot stand in no need of any ideological root cause as their initiation. If anything the ideas, so ardently propounded by men who had received eagerly the current doctrines advocating direct action and workers' control of industry, were given life and root *in the wake* of these immense disturbances. It was defeat in mid-Rhondda that underlined the implacability of the coalowners. It was physical force by police and troops that emphasised the chosen role of the state. It was the half-hearted support accorded to their struggle by their own south Wales miners' leaders that led them to vote well-established figures, including the President of the SWMF from 1898–1912, *Willie Abraham*, Rhondda's MP since 1885, off the Executive Council of the *MFGB*. And it was the conviction of some that leaders

D.18

should *never* be given power if democracy were to have any true meaning that saw the Unofficial Reform Committee formed in 1911 and spread through the coalfield down to 1914.

The single, most important outcome of these particular deliberations was the production of *The Miners' Next Step* in 1912 (D.19). If it had not been published in Tonypandy perhaps *The Times* would not have noticed it sufficiently to denounce in an editorial its allegedly pernicious message of revolt. On the other hand the vigour and power of the pamphlet's content and style would undoubtedly have won it a wide audience across Britain. Its arguments *against* nationalization, *against* trade union bureaucracy, *against* a passive parliamentarianism and *for* a locally rooted democratic structure with, as its objective, the end of all capitalist economies, had, and have, a universal resonance. Its *political* power, though, came precisely from its geographical and industrial context allied to its timing. The authors (six leading militants in Rhondda linked into a wider constituency in south Wales) show that the potential power of the *SWMF* was enormous. Direct action in a one-industry community like south Wales might indeed by-pass the formalized structures of Parliament. There were in 1912 almost 250,000 coalminers in south Wales alone. They had, it was argued, no reason to wait for conciliation between union and employers or to waste energy in sectional disputes they could not win. Centralized, united and with leaders as mere delegates rather than as professional representatives, they could call the tune that would lead on to total control of the industry and, thereby, step by step, bring about a new society.

Success of a kind did come. Leading syndicalists were elected to office. The 1912 minimum wage strike, though not a complete victory in the eyes of militants in south Wales and other coalfields, established the national relevance of the issues at stake in mid-Rhondda in 1910–11. Miners' conferences and miners' agents (white-collar professionalized representatives who often controlled mining districts absolutely) were rattled and almost routed in 1913. Paper resolutions 'to abolish capitalism' were soon enshrined in the *SWMF* Rule Book. Nevertheless, the doctrines of *The Miners' Next Step* were never carried through. It is true their plans for re-organising the

D.19

SWMF on a rank-and-file basis did come about, in a fashion in 1933–4, but that was in a coalfield racked by heavy, long-term unemployment, depleted by mass out-migration and where *the Fed* had been almost smashed by the defeats of the 1920s. *Noah Ablett*, the principal inspiration of that 'syndicalist' generation, died in 1936; his real influence had vanished by the early 1920s.

In November 1912, George Barker, then a miners' agent and later MP for Abertillery, had opposed *Ablett* in a sophisticated debate before a packed house in mid-Rhondda. Barker advocated the attainable objective of a nationalized mining industry
D.20   (D.20). It was soon to be advocated directly by a Government Commission – in 1919. After the devastating run-down of the coal industry in the 1920s and 1930s it came to be seen, by all factions within the miners' union, as a panacea to be desired above all others. It was welcomed as such when it was finally delivered in 1947. The General Secretary of the newly formed National Union of Mineworkers (1944) was, in that year, *Arthur Lewis Horner*, ex-Baptist preacher and elected first Communist President of the SWMF in 1936. *Horner* was the greatest of all the Trade Unionists who emerged from this turbulent coalfield. He was brilliant and committed, as full of integrity as he was skilled in making the best of an unavoidable situation. Nationalization had no greater supporter than *Arthur Horner*. His journey to 1947 is the solution to the equation Tonypandy
D.21   posed (D.21). The riots did raise the spectre of uncontrolled social revolt. They also raised the hopes and fired the minds of those like *Ablett* who, as he said in 1912, saw no way of going forward if people were merely to be led, to be given things, to be
D.20   servile before the bounty of the state (D.20). That revolt was, thereafter, patchy even in south Wales. Compromise, defeat, betrayal, even passivity *are* major elements in the story that unfolded down to 1947. But so is rebellion, heroism, intellectual courage and the resistance of communities to the degradation of a poverty and a way of life not of their making or their choice. It is such choice that is the mark of human liberty above all else. *The Miners' Next Step* concluded with a view of the world when 'mankind shall at last have leisure and inclination to really live as men, and not as the beasts which perish'. *Arthur Horner* lived in the real world in a way the visionary *Noah Ablett* did not but

Horner 'never forgot that lesson'. Tonypandy, 1910, echoes in our history because, in so many ways, it presented men and women, there and elsewhere, with the nature of human choice. It still does.

Sources

D.1   When I was Home Secretary in 1910, I had a great horror and fear of having to become responsible for the military firing on a crowd of rioters or strikers. Also, I was always in sympathy with the miners and I think they are entitled to social dues because they work far from the light of the sun. The Chief Constable of Glamorgan sent a request for the assistance of the military and troops were put in motion in the usual way. But here I made an unprecedented intervention. I stopped the movement of the troops and I sent instead 850 *Metropolitan police* with the sole object of preventing loss of life. I was much criticized for this so-called weakness in the House of Commons, but I carried my point. The troops were kept in the background and all contact with the rioters was made by our trusted and unarmed London police who charged, not with rifles and bayonets but with their rolled-up mackintoshes. Thus all bloodshed, except perhaps some from the nose, was averted, and all loss of life prevented. That is the true story of Tonypandy and I hope it may replace in Welsh villages the cruel lie with which they have been fed all these long years.

(Winston Churchill, General Election campaign 1950, speech in Cardiff, *Western Mail*, 9 February 1950).

D.2   All the Cambrian collieries menaced last night. The Llwynypia Colliery savagely attacked by large crowd of strikers. Many casualties on both sides. Am expecting two companies of infantry and 200 cavalry today . . . Position grave.

(Telegram sent from Lionel Lindsay, Chief Constable of Glamorgan, to the Home Office. Received at 10am on Tuesday, 8 November).

D.3   Your request for military. Infantry should not be used till all other means have failed. Following arrangements have therefore been made. 10 mounted constables and 200 foot constables of *Metropolitan Police* will come to Pontypridd by special train . . . Expect these forces will be sufficient, but as further precautionary measure 200 cavalry will be moved into the district tonight and remain there pending cessation of trouble. Infantry meanwhile will be at Swindon. General Macready will command the military . . . (who) . . . will not however be available unless it is clear that the police reinforcements are unable to cope with the situation.

(Telegram from Churchill to Lindsay, sent at 1.30pm on 8 November).

D.4   Police cannot cope with rioters at Llwynypia, Rhondda Valley. Troops at Cardiff absolutely necessary for further protection. Will you order them to proceed forthwith.

(Telegram from Lleufer Thomas, Stipendiary Magistrate, to the Home Office. Sent at 7.45pm and received at 9pm on 8 November).

D.5   As the situation appears to have become more serious you should if the Chief Constable . . . desires it move all the cavalry into the disturbed district without delay.

(Telegram from Churchill to Macready sent at 8.10pm on 8 November after enquiries had been made by telephone. The magistrate was informed that by the time his telegram had arrived [see above] this request had been met).

D.6   At 1.20am orders were sent to Colonel Currey at Cardiff to despatch the Squadron 18th Hussars at that place so as to reach Pontypridd at 8.15am. On arrival at Pontypridd one squadron patrolled through Aberaman and the other through Llwynypia where it remained during the day in a good position overlooking the Glamorgan colliery . . . At about 5pm I received (further) instructions from the Home Secretary to go to Llwynypia and relieved the 18th Hussars who had been there during the day . . . on their return to Pontypridd (they) arrived at Porth just as a disturbance was breaking out. They held the crowd until the arrival of 50 *Metropolitan foot police* who had been sent from Pontypridd. Major Corbett, 18th Hussars, reported that the crowd showed a rather hostile attitude towards the troops. 300 more *Metropolitan foot police* arrived tonight and will be despatched to Tonypandy.

The troops in the district were billeted as follows during the night.

> 12 Squadrons 18th Hussars at Pontypridd
> 1 Company Royal North Lancashire Regiment at Pontypridd
> 1 Company Lancashire Fusiliers at Llwynypia
> 1 Company West Riding Regiment at Cardiff
> 1 Company Devonshire Regiment at Newport
> 1 Company Royal Munster Fusiliers at Newport.

No disturbance occurred during the night in the district.

(Report by General Macready to the Home Office for 9 November. Troops stationed outside the coalfield were subsequently brought in and on 21 November assisted Metropolitan police in counteracting a violent demonstration by picketing strikers against 'blackleg' workers).

D.7   The last of the mid-Rhondda riots took place on July 25th (1911) at . . . Penygraig . . . The strikers had taken umbrage at the action of certain workmen in accepting employment at the pits of the Naval Company and marched in procession 3,000 strong, towards Penygraig . . . One of the leaders addressed the strikers. He complained that they had been refused permission to see the *blacklegs*, and had been advised to see Mr Llewellyn. But they had had enough of deputations, and were determined to remain there and have an understanding with the *blacklegs* when they came out. By this time, a large proportion of the strikers had got completely out of hand . . . stone throwing became general, and urgent messages were sent to the police headquarters at Tonypandy for reinforcements . . . This force arrived at the Ely colliery soon after . . . and brought the total number of police . . . to over 100. Against between 3,000 and 4,000 desperate rioters spread out along the mountainside, well out of reach of the police and employed in rolling down huge boulders in the direction of the colliery, the police force was hopelessly inadequate, and it became necessary to call in the aid of the military. At 5 o'clock a company of the Somerset Light Infantry, under the command of Major Thickness, surprised the rioters by appearing in extended order on the mountain top armed with fixed bayonets and ball cartridge. They carried their rifles in their hands . . . The troops drove the rioters into the town, where they were charged and dispersed . . . The presence of the military in the district had a decisive influence on the general situation, and after their arrival the police experienced very little difficulty in clearing the streets.

(David Evans, *Labour Strife in the South Wales Coalfield 1910–1911*, 1911, pp.110–111).

D.8   I feel in duty bound to thank you for coming here to restore order . . . on two occasions I have appealed for protection on behalf of those who feared their homes would be ruined by the men who had taken the law into their own hands . . . I think we should be thankful we had special officers sent here to protect our lives and property.

(Statement by a member of mid-Rhondda Free Church Council).

D.9   Immediately after the repulse of the attack on the Glamorgan colliery (on 8th November 1910) came the sack of Tonypandy . . . In their flight from Llwynypia, and under the impression that the victorious police were still at their heels, the rioters, desperate at the defeat of their plans to take the colliery, gave vent to their rage by smashing the windows of every shop that came within reach.

(David Evans, *Labour Strife in the South Wales Coalfield 1910–11*, 1911, p.48).

D.10   Investigations on the spot convinced me that the original reports regarding the attacks on the mines on November 8th had been exaggerated (by the police). What were described as

Troops assembled in Pontypridd in 1910. (*Source: Cyril Batstone.*)

'desperate attempts' to sack the power house at Llwynypia proved to have been an attempt to force the gateway . . . and a good deal of stone throwing . . . and had the mob been as numerous or so determined as the reports implied, there was nothing to have prevented them from overrunning the whole premises. That they did not was due less to the action of the police than to the want of leading or inclination to proceed to extremities on the part of the strikers.

(General Macready, *Annals of an Active Life*, 1924, pp.144–5).

D.11   . . . it was really hell. We had a terrible job . . . driving them back to the Square. Well, we only could get them as far as the Square. On that night, then, that was the night they wrecked all the shops . . . And the whole of the time we could do nothing about it . . . They drove us back every time . . .

(Oral testimony of PC W. Knipe. Transcript in South Wales Miners' Library, Swansea).

D.12   They started smashing the windows . . . they smashed this shop here, J. O. Jones, a *millinery shop* . . . We saw that being smashed and then next door to the *millinery* . . . there was a shop and they smashed the window there . . . on the other side . . . there was Richards the chemist . . . they smashed that. And they smashed the windows of these three small shops here; one was greengrocer, the other one was fancy goods and the other one was a barber's shop . . . and they stole the shoes out of the Boots, flannel out of Watkins and greengrocery, well they only picked up there. Well next to that there was a few steps up and there was a dentist and one or two private houses. Well, they didn't smash – we didn't see anything that happened below the bridge because . . . we were afraid to go down there in front of the crowd . . . oh, there was a huge crowd!

(Oral testimony of Bryn Lewis, an eyewitness of the 1910 riots as a boy. South Wales Miners' Library Transcript).

D.13   People were seen inside the counter handing goods out. They were afterwards walking in the Square wearing various articles of clothing which had been stolen and asking each other how they looked. They were not a bit ashamed, and they actually had the audacity to see how things fitted them in the shop itself. They were in the shop somewhere about three hours and women were as bad as men. Everything was done openly and the din was something horrible.

(Mrs Phillips, Draper, reported in *Draper's Record*, 19th November 1910).

D.14   We deplore the result (of the vote for strike action in later October 1910) because an industrial struggle of this magnitude brings in its train, not only complete disorganisation of the trade of the district . . . but also because of the suffering of those who are no part to the dispute . . . a strike at this period of the year, when trade is looking up and tradesmen are laying in large stores in preparation for the brisk demand, means the withdrawal of a huge sum of money from active circulation in the district.

(*Rhondda Leader*, 29th October, 1910).

D.15   In the last decade of Victoria's reign my optimistic father had opened a grocery shop in the centre of (Clydach Vale's) long main road . . . with several other shops it stood opposite the Central, a massive pub of angry-red brick and dour stone . . . within sight of my father's shop were two Welsh Nonconformist chapels, Noddfa and Libanus (there were five others up and down the Vale), also St Thomas's Church (English), a police station with cells for violent Saturday night men and rioters in strike time, and the Marxian Club . . . A doctor's surgery sent a warning smell out to the pavement night and day.

We lived for years behind and above our busy shop; a living room, pantry and scullery behind, three bedrooms above. It was a 'credit' shop and a history of family fortunes. On a lectern desk panelled with a frosted glass screen lay an enormous black ledger, six inches thick, a double page for each customer. Its chronicle of strike-time debts was my mother's bible and bane . . .

(Rhys Davies's autobiography, *Print of a Hare's Foot*, 1969, pp.8–12).

D.16   A gentleman who is in a big way of business and who owns a very large number of houses and shops estimated his loss well over 1,000. In normal times he received in rental 2,000 a year but his receipts had dropped to about 30 a fortnight.

(*Rhondda Leader*, 24th June, 1911).

D.17   There are . . . cases in respect of whom the inspectors are informed that houses are only obtainable on certain conditions, such as undertaking or promise on the part of the incoming tenant to purchase goods such as furniture or groceries from the owners. Some house-owners . . . object to tenants with many children, while some provision merchants are said to prefer tenants with large families, because every additional child helps to swell the bill for provisions.

(Report of Mr. J. D. Jenkins, Medical Office of Health for Rhondda, July 1911, Rhondda Borough Council Offices).

D.18   The impression conveyed to my mind in regard to the action of the strikers themselves throughout those disturbances, and the motives for rioting, is that the doctrine of extreme socialism preached by a small but energetic section is entirely responsible for the pre-meditated attempts to destroy property.

(General Macready, Memorandum to Home Office, January 1911).

D.19   The year 1910 brought a seeming realisation of this antagonism (between leaders and the rank and file) by the men. Throughout the negotiations for the new agreement, the men continuously insisted more and more on having the controlling voice. Early on it was laid down that plenary powers should not be given to the leaders, but that the final acceptance of any agreement should depend upon the ballot vote of the men . . .

This half-hearted establishment of the principle of direct control by the men found expression again towards the end of the year by the outbreak of the Cambrian and Aberdare disputes. A careful and dispassionate survey of these historic struggles will show that at every stage the interference of leaders prejudiced the case for the men, and also helped to tie their hands in their endeavour to settle the dispute themselves.

To the leaders, everything seemed to be in the melting pot, because the men insisted on taking a hand in the conduct of affairs. There was much vain talk on the leaders' side about 'the growing spirit of anarchy', which was bringing 'chaos' into the coalfield. And on the men's side, a growing distrust of leadership, and a determination to gain more control . . . if measures are not taken to crystallise the new spirit, to give it proper methods in which to function we shall drift back to the old methods of autocracy.

It becomes necessary then to devise means which will enable this new spirit of real democratic control to manifest itself . . .

PROGRAMME

That the organisation (a centralised British union of mine-workers) shall engage in political action, both local and national, on the basis of complete independence of, and hostility to, all capitalist parties, with an avowed policy of wresting whatever advantage it can for the working class . . .

Alliances to be formed, and trades organisation fostered, with a view to steps being taken, to amalgamate all workers into one national and international union, to work for the taking over of all industries, by the workmen themselves.

POLICY

The old policy of identity of interest between employers and ourselves be abolished, and a policy of open hostility installed.

OBJECTIVE

Every industry thoroughly organised . . . to fight, to gain control of, and then to administer, that industry. The co-ordination of all industries on a Central Production Board (to oversee production and distribution according to need) . . . leaving the men themselves to determine under what conditions and how, the work should be done. This would mean real

democracy in real life, making for real manhood and woman-
hood. Any other form of democracy is a delusion and a snare.

(Extracts from *The Miners' Next Step: Being a Suggested Scheme for
the Reorganisation of the Federation,* Tonypandy, 1912).

D.20   Noah Ablett:
     . . . the future does not lie in the direction of bureaucracy. The
roadway to emancipation lies in a different direction than the
offices of a Minister of Mines (operating state nationalisation).
It lies in the democratic organisation, and eventually control of
the industries by the workers themselves in their organised
capacity as trustees for a working-class world. No Minister of
Mines will lead us to our emancipation. That must be the work
of the workers themselves from the bottom upward, and not
from the top downward, which latter means the servile state.
(Applause).

     George Barker:
     . . . I claim we have put before you a feasible proposal for
obtaining the mines of this country, based on a business
proposition (nationalisation through compensation payments
to owners). In opposition to that our friends have put some
revolutionary proposal, which they call an industrial democracy
based on confiscation. Is there any man with a knowledge of the
democracy of this country who believes in the possibility of
getting such a revolution to take place? I challenge our friends
to produce that revolution (laughs). It is no good bringing
German theories from books here. Is there any possibility of any
man going out and persuading the people to take possession of
the mines? No! He would be laughed at as a lunatic. We affirm
again and again that the Nationalisation of Mines Bill is in the
best interest of the workers, aye, and of the nation.

(A Debate on Nationalization v Workers' Control held in
Tonypandy, November, 1912, and (ed. K. O. Morgan) printed
in the *Bulletin of the Society for the Study of Labour History*, No.3,
1975, pp.22–37).

D.21   It was during this period (1910–1911), when my religious hopes were steadily being replaced by ideas of political struggle, that I met *Noah Ablett*, who more than any other man brought me fully into the working-class struggle. From him I learned the wider background to the conditions against which I had instinctively revolted. He was one of the leaders of the Unofficial Reform Committee set up within the *South Wales Miners' Federation*, which in 1912 produced *The Miners' Next Step*, the first coherent programme for a fighting miners' trade union in Wales and a policy based on immediate improvements in the miners' conditions, leading ultimately to working-class control and ownership of the coalfield. That struggle of the miners for the merest minimum standard of living was the background to my early years.

I walked over the mountains (from Merthyr Tydfil) through the night to Tonypandy in November 1910 when we heard that *Winston Churchill* had called out the troops against the miners. The Tonypandy incident followed the strike of 15,000 men employed in the Cambrian group of pits against the scandalous *piece work* rates imposed on the men at the coal face. The rate varied from district to district and even from mine to mine, but the biggest grievance arose because a man would find himself unable to get enough coal even to produce the miserable subsistence wage. He might be assigned to a place where the seam wall was crushed into small coal, which in South Wales at that time was not paid for at all. He might have to put in exceptional timbering to prevent dangerous falls, and the management, knowing that he was not getting good coal, would not keep him supplied with enough trams to take away what he had hewed so that whatever skill or hard work the man put in, he could still find himself with practically no earnings at all. In some of the pits the men used to cast lots for place. The men at that time were demanding a prescribed minimum of daily earnings for all *piece workers*, and with the resistance of the coal owners these flared up into disputes all over the Aberdare and Rhondda valleys.

When I reached Tonypandy the rioting had been going on all through the night. All the shop fronts were smashed. It has begun after the owners had attempted, on 6th and 7th

November, to bring *blackleg* labour to man the pumps and ventilators at Glamorgan colliery, Llwynypia. The strikers surrounded the colliery. The police were rushed to the pit and on the following day used truncheons to disperse demonstrators . . . During the clash, some shops were damaged, and there was some looting.

It was after this that *Winston Churchill*, who was Home Secretary at the time, ordered men of the Lancashire Fusiliers, the 18th Hussars and the West Riding Regiment to reinforce the thousands of police already in the area. I saw in action that day the vicious alliance of the Government and the coal owners, backed by police and armed troops, against miners who asked no more than a wage little over starvation level. I never forgot that lesson.

(Arthur Horner in his autobiography, *Incorrigible Rebel* 1960, pp.15–16).

Debating the Evidence

David Smith has provided a wide range of documents which bring out many of the strengths and weaknesses in written evidence. Essentially, the questions which historians need to ask of such documents are similar whatever they are. However, the strengths and weaknesses of the direct and indirect evidence yielded by autobiography, Home Office telegrams, newspapers and a coalfield manifesto of action are going to vary greatly. To take just one example, when Home Secretary *Winston Churchill* says, in an official Home Office telegram in 1910, 'Ten mounted constables and 200 foot constables of *Metropolitan Police* will come to Pontypridd by special train . . .' we can be sure that these arrangements have been made. However, *Churchill*'s statement, made in 1950, in public in an election address, that 'All bloodshed, except perhaps some from the nose, was averted', is evidence of a different kind and needs to be analysed differently even though it emanates from the same person as the telegram.

Source D.1

1. Is this a primary or a secondary source? You will need to refer to the Introduction before answering this question. And even then it is not easy to come to a conclusion. Argue the case for it being primary, then

THE WAR OFFICE AND THE CAVALRY.

ORDERS FOR THE MEN TO BE DETAINED AT CARDIFF.

TO BE READY IN CASE THEIR PRESENCE SHOULD BE WANTED!!

ONE SQUADRON LEAVES FOR THE RHONDDA.

METROPOLITAN POLICE SENT ON TO PONTYPRIDD.

The following official statement was issued from the Home Office on Tuesday night:—

A request was addressed last night by the chief-constable of Glamorgan to the local military authorities for the assistance of 200 cavalry and two companies of infantry in keeping order in the Cambrian Collieries.

The Home Secretary, in consultation with Mr. Haldane, decided to send instead a contingent of the Metropolitan police, consisting of 70 mounted and 200 foot constables, to the district to carry out the instructions of the chief-constable, under their own officers. This force was sent by special trains, and will arrive in the early evening.

In the meanwhile, the cavalry and infantry which had been despatched in response to the chief-constable's request have with his concurrence, been detained—the infantry at Swindon and the cavalry at Cardiff, where they will remain for a few days in case their presence should prove to be necessary.

CAVALRY AT CARDIFF.

ANIMATED SCENES AT THE RAILWAY STATION.

The Great Western Railway station at Cardiff on Tuesday evening presented the appearance of an Army headquarters on a miniature scale. From 6.30 on military officers were arriving by train from various parts of the country and at once proceeding to the stationmaster's office, where Brigadier-general C. F. N. Macready, C.B., was in constant telegraphic and telephonic communication with the War Office and the chief-constable of Glamorgan (Captain Lindsay). The general came down from London in the afternoon, arriving at Cardiff by the 6.15 p.m. train. With him was Colonel M. C. Curry, D.A.G. and they were met by Lieutenant-colonel E. A. T. Phillips, R.G.A., commanding the troops in the Cardiff district, and Captain Bennette, A.S.C., Pembroke Dock.

A quarter of an hour prior to the general's arrival a squadron of the 18th Hussars, with their horses, arrived at the Great Western Railway station from Salisbury Plain and those were at once despatched to the Canton sidings, where they remained in the train until 6.30, when they detrained and marched to the Cardiff Barracks, where they put up for the night. Their sudden appearance at Cardiff caused some excitement among the station officials, who understood the significance of the soldiers' arrival.

The general officer commanding seemed to be in some considerable doubt as to giving such an aspect that another contingent of any definite orders for the sending of the troops up to the scene of operations, and it seemed evident that he was not in possession of the serious aspect affairs had assumed.

It was difficult to ascertain the identity of

the officers arriving by each train. They all immediately waited upon General Macready, and at one time eight were in the stationmaster's room, the consultation lasting until eight o'clock. A quartermaster-sergeant of the Welsh Regiment from Cardiff Barracks was in attendance the whole time, and there were also a number of orderlies.

The railway officials were also present in full force, among them being Mr. J. J. Lansing, divisional superintendent, Mr. J. Carter, assistant divisional superintendent; Mr Hulin, the stationmaster, &c., while an interested attendant was Mr. C. A. G. Pullin, Mr. B. A. Thomas's private secretary.

When the Hussars arrived the orders for the officer commanding were that he must not proceed further than Cardiff until he received a communication from the War Office. He was also informed by telegram that General Macready was on his way from London to command operations.

It was very evident that even General Macready was under orders not to proceed further than Cardiff until receiving instructions from the War Office.

By the 7.30 train another batch of officers arrived from Bristol, and after acquainting the general of the fact they left the station.

At 8.5 the first contingent consisting of 150 foot police arrived from London. These men were under the charge of Superintendent Powell, and an hour and a half later a special arrived with 100 men and their horses. These forces were immediately despatched to Pontypridd, where further orders awaited them.

CAVALRY LEAVE FOR THE RHONDDA.

ALL FURNISHED WITH BALL AMMUNITION.

A squadron of the 18th Hussars arrived at Cardiff at 11.15, they having left Tidworth at 6.45. On Major Burnett, who was in command, reporting himself to Colonel Curry, who was in charge—General Macready having left earlier for Pontypridd—he was ordered to leave at once for Pontypridd, where further orders awaited him. The train left at 11.30. The men were all furnished with ball ammunition, and are prepared for any eventuality.

MORE LONDON POLICE.

The situation during the evening assumed such an aspect that another contingent of police were telegraphed for from London, and they arrived at Cardiff Station at three o'clock this morning. An engine of the Taff Vale Company, with officials, was immediately attached to the train, and it proceeded up to the Rhondda.

Report in the *Western Mail*, 9 November 1910. (*Source: National Library of Wales.*)

argue the case for it being secondary. Then turn to document D.21 and consider whether document D.21 is a primary or secondary source.

2. Why is the distinction between primary and secondary evidence an important one?

3. What motives might *Churchill* have had here in making the case that he acted with unprecedented moderation in Tonypandy?

Source D.3

How does the evidence in this document square with *Churchill*'s statement in Source D.1?

Source D.4

What true statement about the Tonypandy riots could a historian make on the basis of this document, given the fact that it is a genuine document and not a forgery?

Source D.5

How does the evidence in this document square with *Churchill*'s statement in Source D.1?

Source D.6

1. How much credence would you give to the information in this document? Why?

2. Would you expect Macready to give inaccurate information to the Home Office? Why?

3. Would you expect Macready to give biased information to the Home Office? Why?

Source D.7

Present-day historians generally accept that David Evans gave a one-sided account of the events in Tonypandy. Is there any evidence in this passage as to which side he favoured?

Source D.12

Bryn Lewis was recorded in the 1970s. He was a witness to the riots in 1910. What are the strengths and weaknesses of this source?

Source D.14

What information would you need to have about the ownership, management, production and circulation of the *Rhondda Leader* before making proper use of this source?

Source D.15

Explain the relevance of this source to the topic of the Tonypandy riots.

Source D.18

1. What further information would you require before being able to evaluate the worth of this source?
2. What valid historical statement could you make without having any further information?

Source D.19

What briefly is the case being argued here?

Source D.21

1. On the evidence of this document, would you regard *Arthur Horner* as being in a good or bad position to write about the Tonypandy riots? Why?
2. What evidence in the *Horner* extract is corroborated *or* contradicted by evidence in the other documents in this section?

Discussion

You have just completed a variety of exercises on written sources, exercises which varied between the straightforward and the complex. Source D.1 immediately highlights some of the problems which historians face. *Churchill* was in a unique position to inform posterity about central government's policy in Tonypandy. Yet the pressures on him, or any politician, to portray his actions in the most favourable light were immense, then and later. His own reputation was at stake. Every politician wishes it to be acknowledged that he did the right thing at a moment of crisis, and *Churchill* did not enjoy the highest of reputations for cool appraisal of events, especially before the Second World War. The pressures on *Churchill* by 1950 were far greater. First, despite being a national hero in 1945 he had been voted out of office at his moment of triumph. To say that he was anxious to be back in Downing Street is a major understatement. Second, by 1950, he knew full well that he was a prisoner of the myth of Tonypandy. It was no myth that he had authorised sending troops there. Document D.5 is unequivocal on this. However, the historian would argue that to pin the blame solely on *Churchill* would be to ignore both the pressures on him (Document D.4) and his attempt to keep the military out (Document D.3). *Churchill* actually seems to have been hurt by the reputation which he never failed to live down.

There are other difficulties with this document, because *Churchill* was recalling events of forty years before. He might have had 'total recall'; but his memory is more likely to have clouded over this timespan.

So, what is most striking about the document is the complexity of interpreting it. All such documents are biased, but the bias is not simple. It is by no means just a case of saying that *Churchill* was cynically determined, for electoral reasons, to provide an interpretation favourable to himself. In fact the document is particularly interesting for what it might be telling us about *Churchill* as well as the information it gives us about events in Tonypandy. Documents D.2 to D.5 reinforce the notion of *Churchill*'s evidence being far from simple to interpret. At one level we are much nearer answering the equally valid historical question: does he deserve his enduring reputation as the man who sent troops to subdue Tonypandy?

It is beginning to look as if we cannot be sure of anything in historical documents. If this were the case there would be no point in having primary sources and there would be no worthwhile history. We know from Document D.4, for example, that Lleufer Thomas, the *stipendiary magistrate*, on 8 November 1910, requested the Home Office to order troops to be sent from Cardiff to control rioting at Llwynypia. There is some unintentional information here too – that there was a *stipendiary magistrate*, that the Home Office had to authorize the deployment of troops. But it is important to remember that virtually everything else here needs to be treated with caution. It is almost certain, from the document, that Lleufer Thomas thought that the police could not cope with the rioting. But he *could* have panicked and genuinely exaggerated the danger. He *could* have had an ulterior motive for wanting the troops in the Rhondda Valley.

Then there is the problem of language. Historians rarely use a specialised vocabulary. The use of ordinary language, paradoxically, poses problems. It is not neutral. One observer's '*blackleg*' might be another's 'company employee'. In D.7 David Evans uses some evocative phrases. Strikers had 'taken umbrage'; strikers had 'got completely out of hand'; rioters were 'desperate'. How big were those 'huge boulders' being rolled down the mountainside? How many is 'between 3,000 and 4,000' – and how many police is 'over 100'? In Document D.9 we have 'the sack of Tonypandy'.

There are many events of the last two centuries for which the only evidence available is in newspapers. Because of their frequency of publication they are invaluable; but the use of the *Rhondda Leader* in connection with the Tonypandy riots is fraught with difficulty, whether we are using the reporting or the editorials. It would appear from the extracts included here that the interests which the paper represented were those of the Rhondda shopkeepers. We would do well, perhaps, to correlate our investigation of ownership and management with a close study of the advertisements which the paper carried. It was certainly a paper which supported the Liberal consensus view of politics rather than that epitomized in *The Miners' Next Step*.

The sources section ends, as it begins, with an eye-witness recalling many years later the experience of the time. This source, like the first, highlights the problems – and the fascination – of trying to evaluate primary sources of historical evidence.

David Lloyd George, 1903. (*Source: BBC Hulton Picture Library.*)

David Lloyd George and Wales

KENNETH O. MORGAN

Between 1880 and 1914, David Lloyd George came to be regarded as the symbol and tribune of the national reawakening of Wales. More than any other politician, indeed more than anyone else alive, he seemed to embody the aspirations, frustrations, legends and dreams of the Welsh people. The resurgence of Liberalism in the late nineteenth and early twentieth centuries, the new style of popular politics, the national demands being voiced in parliamentary and local affairs, the fresh impact that Wales was making upon the consciousness of its English neighbour and a wider world – all these were uniquely identified with Lloyd George's dramatic progress from the backwoods of Llanystumdwy in southern Llŷn in the 1880s into parliament in 1890 and from 1905 onwards into the British cabinet. This association of Welsh political nationhood with his career did not come to an end with the outbreak of world war in 1914, or the subsequent collapse of the Liberal Party which was one of its major dramatic consequences. During the war years and afterwards, he continued to use Welshness and its political manifestations as major support in his campaigns to retain, or regain, power. Contemporaries long after the war continued to define Welshness largely in terms of Lloyd George's style and outlook.

The economist, *J. M. Keynes*, in a book published in 1933, attributed many of the defects of the *Treaty of Versailles* in 1919 to the Welsh manoeuvrings of a chameleon-like prime minister who had emerged mysteriously 'from the hag-ridden magic and enchanted woods of Celtic antiquity'. This identification continued until Lloyd George's death in 1945. Of course, as will be seen, Lloyd George's relation to Welsh politics was far from straightforward. In some respects, he was out of sympathy with the nature of middle-class Nonconformist radicalism as it developed in late-Victorian Wales. Even so, to examine Lloyd George's activities, and some of the manuscripts and printed historical sources that exist to help us to trace them, in the period 1880–1914 takes us close to many of the driving themes in Welsh history in these critical years. It leads us to explore central aspects of the very essence of Welsh nationhood, then and later.

Lloyd George's involvement in politics began young. His earliest memories of political life came at the age of five, during the great general election of 1868 (E.1), which saw so many remarkable Liberal victories, followed after the polls by the politically-motivated eviction of several tenant farmers in Caernarfonshire by their landlords for having voted Liberal. Forty-two years on, during the campaign for the *People's Budget* when Lloyd George was now *Chancellor*, he was to recall the memories and oral tradition of these remote but still stirring events. His childhood years were scarred by frequent political tensions – resentment at the *Tory* landlords who dominated the countryside, and at the Anglican Church which made young Nonconformist children like the Baptist Lloyd George attend Church schools. His political ambitions were fanned by his uncle, Richard Lloyd, the radical shoemaker who brought him up after his father died. It was natural that in the young boy's first visit to London in 1880, at the age of 17, a major impression was that made by the spectacle (if not, apparently, the architecture) of the House of Commons (E.2). Soon he was embroiled in local political affairs, including the local Portmadoc debating club, and some youthful involvement in local newspapers – always a key to his career and political methods. His chosen career as a country solicitor was an ideal base for a future political life. Nothing would be allowed to stand in the way of his destiny. When he began courting Maggie Owen of Mynydd Ednyfed farm around 1885 (E.3), she was told at an early stage that even love itself must give way to the 'Juggernaut' of his fate and his 'supreme idea to get on'. In the 1886 general election, which saw the Liberal Party funda-

E.1

E.2

E.3

mentally split over *Irish home rule*, Lloyd George was actively involved. He spoke successfully at a famous meeting before the slate quarrymen of Blaenau Ffestiniog with the Irish Nationalist leader, *Michael Davitt*, early that year. After some hesitation, he came down decisively in favour of *Gladstone* in his crusade for Irish self-government. Lloyd George also involved himself in the '*tithe war*' by north Wales tenant farmers who refused to pay *tithe* to the Church in the 1886–8 period. His outlook was decidedly on the political left, and strongly influenced by the Welsh national sentiment surging through the land in the later

E.4   1880s. He told a Caernarfonshire friend, *D. R. Daniel* (E.4), that he regarded himself as a 'Welsh Nationalist' of the same type as the young Merioneth MP, *Tom Ellis*. He was elected to the first Caernarfonshire county council in 1889 and became very vocal in the affairs of the newly formed North Wales and South Wales Liberal *Federations*. In a major speech to the SWLF in February

E.5   1890 (E.5), he spelt out the usual Liberal priorities – *disestablishment* of the Church, land reform, temperance reform – together with a striking emphasis on social questions and the remedy of mass poverty. At the age of just 27 he was clearly a coming man. His career received a massive boost in April 1890 when he was elected Liberal MP for Caernarfon Boroughs. He was to retain it for 55 years; yet it was anything but a safe seat at first. It had been won by the Conservatives in 1886 and Lloyd George captured it back by just an 18-vote majority. His election campaign had been uncomplicated in its radicalism. He had endorsed all the main lines of *Gladstonian Liberalism* (E.6),

E.6   including *Irish home rule*, but with also a heavy emphasis on Welsh themes, headed by 'Religious Liberty', a code for Welsh *disestablishment*. This was a dangerous line to take, especially in Bangor with its cathedral and Church vote. In early June, he

E.7   made his maiden speech (E.7). It was a typically rumbustuous affair with a heavy Welsh stress on the temperance question; he boasted cheerfully to his wife about its success. He soon emerged as a backbench gadfly on Welsh issues in the Commons. He urged his older colleagues to put more pressure on *Gladstone* and the Liberal leadership on behalf of Church

E.8   *disestablishment* (E.8). He also took an active part in the debates on the *Tithe Act* of 1891, a measure designed to placate the angry Welsh farmers who had taken part in the *tithe* disturbances. 'It was a glorious struggle for Wales', in Lloyd George's view (E.9). Returned with a larger majority in 1892, he continued to take an aggressive role in pressing the various radical causes of Wales. With three backbench colleagues, he even led a brief revolt against the party whip in April 1894, when the government failed to give a sufficiently high priority to Welsh *disestablishment* in its legislative programme. This caused much rancour for a time, since the government's majority was barely 20 and that dependent on Irish Nationalist votes. Yet the general impression he created at this time in parliament was a positive one. Even a political opponent like the Unionist writer, *T. Marchant Williams* (E.10), could see Lloyd George already as an outstanding debater and parliamentary tactician. He was a potential leader of the Welsh MPs in the Commons and – who knew? – even of the Liberal Party as a whole. Further controversy surrounded his activities in the 1895 session. The government had not introduced a Welsh *Disestablishment* Bill, which he of course supported. But he now tried to use this measure as a lever for forcing through a kind of Welsh home rule. In June 1895 he and two other Welsh members were involved in trying to get through a Welsh national council to administer *tithe* and other endowments when the Welsh Church Bill became law. On 20 June, the government's majority fell to two; the next day, on a snap vote, the government resigned office. In the general election in July, the Liberals were heavily defeated, and Lloyd George did well to hang on to his shaky seat at Caernarfon Boroughs. After the election, therefore, his activities in May–June 1895 came under fire. *Bryn Roberts*, the Liberal MP for neighbouring North Caernarfonshire, who had no sympathy for either Lloyd George or Welsh home rule, had written to *Asquith*, the Home Secretary, on 18 May, warning him about Lloyd George's freelance nationalist tactics (E.11). In November, *Asquith* himself complained to *Tom Ellis*, now the Liberal chief whip, about Lloyd George's 'underhand and disloyal' behaviour the previous June (E.12). *Ellis* and other Liberals defended their young colleague, but the memory of these events was to haunt the *Asquith*–Lloyd George relationship long into the future.

Tom Ellis, Liberal MP for Merioneth. (*Source: National Library of Wales.*)

The pivotal episode in Lloyd George's involvement in Welsh politics came with the *Cymru Fydd* (Young Wales) crisis in 1895–6. His Welsh nationalism was now at its most intense. He felt convinced that the only logical way for Wales to obtain *disestablishment*, land reform and her other prized objectives was to achieve her own government within a federal imperial system. The progress made by *Irish home rule* encouraged some to believe that Welsh and Scottish home rule might well follow on. Throughout 1895 Lloyd George tried to turn the North and South Wales Liberal *Federations* into organs for Welsh nationalism by merging them with his own *Cymru Fydd* League. The NWLF was won over easily enough. Lloyd George spent much time and ingenuity in the summer and autumn of 1895 in trying to win over the South Wales Liberals as well. In Tredegar, in anglicized Monmouthshire for instance, he claimed to find an excellent response, even though the local populace was sunk in a 'morbid footballism' (E.13). But the anglicized, industrialized population of south-east Wales, especially the great cosmopolitan ports of Swansea, Barry, Cardiff and Newport, were deeply suspicious. As in the devolution campaign in 1979, they feared coming under the domination of the Welsh-speaking population of the rural hinterland. The climax came with the disastrous meeting of the South Wales Liberal *Federation* in Newport on 16 January 1896. Here Lloyd George was howled down, and *Cymru Fydd* denounced by the mercantile representatives of south-east Wales. He claimed to his wife and his Flintshire friend, *Herbert Lewis*, MP (E.14, E.15), that the Newport meeting was packed and unrepresentative, and that the fight for Welsh home rule would go on. Yet it was a decisive watershed in his career, the first rebuff he had yet encountered. It dawned upon him that while Welsh Liberals were firm for Church *disestablishment*, land reform, education and temperance, and for national equality within the British Isles, they did not want separatism. The Welsh were just not like the Irish. They did not want to be cut off from England or from the imperial system. Welsh home rule was, in effect, struck off the political agenda, perhaps for ever, and Lloyd George recognized the fact. He would fight for a losing cause but not for a lost one. In 1896 as in 1979, the Welsh people, when offered a prospect of

E.13

E.14
E.15

some political self-determination, rejected it out of hand by a decisive margin.

After the *Cymru Fydd* debacle, Lloyd George's relationship with Welsh politics became somewhat more indirect. His countrymen now acknowledged his talents as a Liberal front-bench spokesman: thus *Llewelyn Williams*, another nationalist lawyer, praised Lloyd George's parliamentary skills in August E.16   1896 (E.16). Lloyd George continued to hammer home the needs of Wales in debates on agricultural rating and education. But there were signs of wider interests and broader horizons. In Wales, the veteran editor, *Thomas Gee* of the *Faner*, Lloyd George's ally over the years, died in 1898; the following year, *Tom Ellis* died of tuberculosis at the age of 39. The leaders and, indirectly, the issues of Welsh life were changing. So it was with David Lloyd George. The change was dramatically registered with the outbreak of war in South Africa in October 1899. Lloyd George was by no means hostile to the idea of empire then or later. But his attitude towards the war in South Africa was consistent and courageous from the start. He felt certain that waging war upon two small Boer republics, run by Calvinist farmers rather like the Welsh, was a political and moral wrong. The cause lay, he claimed, in the political ambitions and financial interests of *Joseph Chamberlain*, the Colonial Secretary. As early as 27 October 1899, he delivered a stinging attack upon the great *Chamberlain* which stunned the House of Commons E.17   (E.17). He kept up the attack for the rest of the war, which dragged on until May 1902. He needed all his courage in the face of violent mobs in Glasgow and in Birmingham Town Hall, and even in his own constituency in Bangor and Caernarfon. He only just hung on to his seat in the '*khaki election*' of October 1900. But gradually public opinion began to turn and the Liberal Party became increasingly hostile to the methods and purpose of the imperial war in South Africa. One great result was the new national stature for Lloyd George himself. As an admiring Liberal journalist, Harold Spender, wrote in 1901 E.18   (E.18), Lloyd George had advanced from being just a back-bench spokesman for Welsh radicalism to becoming a figure admired and feared throughout the land. The highest office seemed within his grasp.

But his involvement in Welsh politics remained central in his career even after the *Boer War*. When the prime minister, *Arthur Balfour*, introduced a great *Education Act* in 1902, Lloyd George led the resistance of Welsh Liberals. His initial reaction to the act was far from hostile; but like other Liberals he resented its imposing Church elementary schools, the only schools in many 'single school areas', as an unrequited burden upon Welsh Nonconformist ratepayers. In a meeting of the Welsh MPs in November 1902, he persuaded them to accept an amendment which would make the Welsh county councils the instruments

E.19 for operating the Act in the principality (E.19). That gave him a powerful platform from which to launch a counter-attack. By early 1904, all the Welsh county councils, every one of which now had a Liberal majority, were united in resisting the operation of the *Education Act*, a kind of mass strike by the Welsh local authorities. For three years, 1902–5, there was a complete impasse between Wales and Whitehall. But, as ever, Lloyd George used the opportunity to push on beyond narrow sectarian issues into wider national directions. As he told the Scottish journalist, William Robertson Nicoll, editor of the

E.20 *British Weekly* (E.20), he was trying to use his position of strength to coerce the leaders of the Welsh Church into accepting a compromise over Church schools. Another outcome could be a Welsh Educational Board to promote a uniform elementary and secondary system of schooling throughout Wales, and to serve as a pioneer of future devolution. In the end, his efforts failed. The forces of sectarian conflict were too deep-rooted for him. There were those like his fellow Liberal *Arthur Humphreys-Owen*, MP for Montgomeryshire, who criticized Lloyd George, with his limited educational background, for using the nation's schools for purely political

E.21 ends (E.21). Yet the affair of the education 'revolt' further enhanced Lloyd George's reputation for constructive statesmanship. There were other critics who noted gaps in his understanding. The *Independent Labour Party* newspaper, *Labour Leader*, observed that his enthusiasm for religious or political issues was not matched by any similar concern for industrial or

E.22 social questions (E.22). Lloyd George, who had largely ignored even the massive six-months coal lock-out in south Wales in

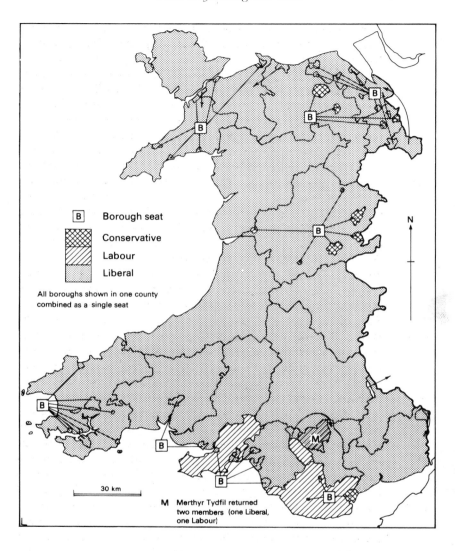

Legend:

B Borough seat

Conservative

Labour

Liberal

All boroughs shown in one county
combined as a single seat

N

30 km

M Merthyr Tydfil returned
two members (one Liberal,
one Labour)

General Election Result, 1910 (based on Madgwick and Balsom, *National Atlas of Wales*.)

1898, 'had practically nothing to say for Labour'. But these themes lay in the future. In January 1906, fortified by the Education 'revolt', Lloyd George and the Liberal Party swept the board. Not one *Tory* was returned for the 34 Welsh seats. All, save *Keir Hardie*'s position as junior member for Merthyr, were in Liberal hands.

Lloyd George was now a political figure on the British stage. From December 1905 to April 1908 he served in the Cabinet as President of the Board of Trade, with great success. Thereafter, until the war, he went to the Treasury as the most powerful and creative Chancellor of the Exchequer in modern British history.

His concern with Welsh affairs was inevitably more episodic. One of them was in trying to calm down Welsh Nonconformists who complained to the prime minister, *Sir Henry Campbell-Bannerman* in 1907, that nothing was being done to promote Welsh *disestablishment* (E.23). This crisis passed, but in fact a Welsh *disestablishment* bill did not appear on the government's legislative programme in settled form until April 1912. The main theme in Lloyd George's career, as far as Wales and Britain generally was concerned henceforth, was social reform. As has been seen (E.5) this had figured in some early speeches, though in sketchy form. When speaking to the Welsh National Liberal Council in Cardiff in October 1906 (E.24), he still emphasized the old questions of *disestablishment*, land reform and temperance for the working men of Wales. But when he went to the Treasury in April 1908, his outlook, like that of his friend, *Winston Churchill*, greatly changed. When he spoke to the Welsh Liberals again at Swansea in October 1908 (E.25), his emphasis was now on social measures as desirable both in themselves and to beat off the challenge to Liberalism posed by the Labour Party. Down to 1914, it was social welfare that inspired much of his effort – *Old Age Pensions* in 1908; the *People's Budget* in 1909; the historic passage of *National Health insurance* and some unemployment insurance in 1911; frequent negotiations with the trade unions to ward off strikes and promote social justice. By 1914 he was the dominant figure in the government, the most celebrated Welshman of the age. An old Liberal like *Lord Rendel* (E.26) continued to admire his democratic, egalitarian attitude. His own hostility to privilege and the establishment in whatever form continued to show itself. When he visited King George V at Balmoral in 1911, he hated the atmosphere – 'it reeks with *Toryism*' (E.27). In August 1914, his radical zeal was still undiminished as was the continued enthusiasm for him amongst most classes and groups in his native land.

E.27

This self-contained phase of Lloyd George's career came to an abrupt end on 4th August 1914. Thereafter, his life took a very different turn. He became Minister of Munitions in 1915, Secretary of State for War in 1916, Prime Minister from December 1916 to October 1922. At home he was now the ally of the *Tories*, hated by many on the left, his own Liberal Party divided and in ruins. Abroad, for a time in 1919–22, he was the supreme peacemaker and architect of a new Europe and a new world order. His relations with Wales were never quite the same. He had tried to appeal to Welsh national sentiment on behalf of the 'little five-foot-five nations' during the war (E.28) but it rebounded against him afterwards. From 1922 he was out of power for ever, rejected even by the voters of Wales where Labour was now dominant. Lloyd George himself remained in parliament and an influential voice in economic and foreign affairs; but by the time of his death in March 1945 even Wales's great commoner had become an earl. It is in the years 1880–1914 that his main influence on Welsh history can be detected. It is clear that here, in Welsh as in British society, he was a maverick, an outsider. He was never much of a cultural nationalist. He had scant interest in the national passion for education. He favoured compromise and coalitions in a manner all his own. He felt deep contempt for the 'glorified grocers' of Liberalism and the 'big seats' of the chapels. In his private and public life, he was certainly no puritan (E.29). Yet in his younger period he did more to advance the causes of Wales in public life than any other man. Apart from Welsh church *disestablishment* in 1920, improvements in the land, educational advance and social reforms, there were cultural achievements such as the university, the National Library and National Museum of Wales, the *Welsh Department of the Board of Education*. All were part of the Liberal heritage of pre-1914; all had some connection, direct or indirect, with Lloyd George's campaigns. To the end, he retained a fierce sense of national identity, of an un-English

E.28

E.29

Lloyd George's funeral, Llanystumdwy, 1945. (*Source: National Library of Wales.*)

separateness. As late as 1936, when he was holidaying in Jamaica, he wrote angrily to his daughter, Megan, now Liberal MP for Anglesey, about the government's bullying of Wales by the mishandling of the case of *Saunders Lewis*, a Welsh nationalist who had set fire to an RAF bombing school in Llŷn
E.30   (E.30). To the end, Lloyd George could be the unremitting champion of 'gallant little Wales'. If Welsh self-government did not crown his efforts, that was hardly his fault. The cause lay deep in the roots of the Welsh as a people. He did more than any of his contemporaries to make Wales a political and social reality, and a dignified member of a wider world.

Sources

E.1   After the election notices to quit were showered upon the tenants. What happened? They were turned out by the score on to the roadside because they dared to vote according to their consciences. But they woke the spirit of the mountains, the genius of freedom that fought the might of the Normans for two centuries. There was such a feeling aroused amongst the people that, ere it was done, the political power of landlordism in Wales was shattered, as effectually as the power of the Druids. It is my first memory of politics, and that is why I am proud to be President of the *Gladstone* League.

(Lloyd George, speech at Queen's Hall, London, 23rd March 1910, *The Times*, 24 March, 1910).

E.2   Went to Houses of Parliament – very much disappointed with them. Grand buildings outside but inside they are crabbed, small and suffocating, especially House of Commons. I will not say but that I eyed the assembly in a spirit similar to that in which William the Conqueror eyed England on his visit to Edward the Confessor, the region of his future domain. Oh, vanity.

(Lloyd George, diary entry, Saturday, 12th November 1880, W. R. P. George, *The Making of Lloyd George*, London, 1976, p.101).

E.3   It comes to this. My supreme idea is to get on. To this idea I shall sacrifice everything – except I trust honesty. I am prepared to thrust even love itself under the wheels of my Juggernaut, if it obstructs the way, that is if love is so much trumpery child's play as your mother deems courtship to be. I have told you over and over that I consider you to be my good angel – my guiding star. Do you not really desire my success? If you do, will you suggest some course least objectionable to you out of our difficulty? I am prepared to do anything reasonable & fair you may require of me. I can not – earnestly – carry on as present. Believe me – & may Heaven attest the truth of my statement – my love for you is sincere & strong. In this I never waver. But I must not forget that I have a purpose in life. And however painful the sacrifice I may have to make to attain this ambition I must not flinch – otherwise success will be remote indeed . . .

(Lloyd George to Miss Margaret Owen, ? 1885, National Library of Wales, Aberystwyth, Lloyd George Papers).

E.4 You know that I am a Welsh Nationalist of the *Ellis* type. Have *more or less* thoroughly studied the Church, land and temperance questions.

(Lloyd George to D. R. Daniel, 5th July 1888, National Library of Wales, Aberystwyth, Daniel Papers).

E.5 We have never quarrelled with tyranny as the Irish have done. We have rather turned the other cheek to the smiter . . . This resolution is a fitting climax to this meeting's programme. You have pledged yourselves to – *Disestablishment*, Land Reform, Local Option and other great reforms. But, however drastic and broad they may appear to be, they after all simply touch the fringe of that vast social question which must be dealt with in the near future. There is a momentous time coming. The dark continent of wrong is being explored and there is a missionary spirit abroad for its reclamation to the realm of right. That is why I feel so sanguine that were self-government granted to Wales she would be a model to the nationalities of the earth of a people who have driven oppression from their hillsides, and initiated the glorious reign of freedom, justice and truth.

(Lloyd George, speech to South Wales Liberal Federation, February 1890, W. R. P. George, *op. cit.*, p.166).

E.6   Recent by-elections prove that the country is sick and tired of
       Mr *Balfour*'s baton-and-bayonet rule in Ireland, and of his
       desperate attempts to repress by martial law legitimate aspira-
       tions of a generous nation. I come before you as a firm believer
       in and admirer of Mr *Gladstone*'s noble alternative of Justice to
       Ireland. Whilst fully recognizing that the wrongs of Ireland
       must of necessity have the first claim upon the attention of the
       Liberal party, I am deeply impressed with the fact that Wales has
       wants and inspirations of her own which have too long been
       ignored, but which must no longer be neglected. First and
       foremost amongst these stands the cause of Religious Liberty
       and Equality in Wales. If returned to Parliament by you, it shall
       be my earnest endeavour to labour for the triumph of this great
       cause. I believe in a liberal extension of the principle of
       Decentralization. There are also such questions as 'One Man
       One Vote', Graduated Taxation, 'A Free Breakfast Table', and
       many another much-needed Reform; but what availeth it even
       to enumerate them while there is a *Tory* Government in power?

       (From Lloyd George's election address, Caernarfon Boroughs
       by-election, April 1890, H. du Parcq, *Life of David Lloyd George*,
       I, London, 1912, pp.95, 96).

E.7   Shortly after I wrote my letter of yesterday to you I got up &
       spoke for the first time in the House of Commons . . . There is
       no doubt I scored a success & a great one. The old man &
       Trevelyan [Sir G. O. Trevelyan (1838–1928): Liberal MP],
       Morley, [John Morley (1836–1923): Liberal MP], *Harcourt*
       appeared delighted. I saw Morley afterwards & he said it was a
       'capital speech – *first rate*' & he said so with marked emphasis.
       He is such a dry stick that he wouldn't have said anything unless
       he thoroughly believed it. I have been overwhelmed with
       congratulations both yesterday & today. *Tom Ellis* who is
       genuinely delighted because one of his own men has succeeded
       – told me that several members had congratulated *Wales* upon
       my speech. *Stuart Rendel* said I had displayed 'very distinguished
       powers'. There is hardly a London Liberal or even a provincial
       paper which does not say something commendatory about it.

       (Lloyd George to Mrs Lloyd George, 14th June 1890, National
       Library of Wales, Aberystwyth).

E.8   The Welsh party met on Tuesday to discuss *Disestablishment* & elaborately resolved to do nothing. They met last night to discuss the *G.O.M.*'s letter & unhesitatingly determined to take action in advance of all other sections in support of 'their great leader'. That's *Rendelism*. We, the younger lot, are inclined to grumble at this. Unfortunately, at this juncture it is impossible to get up any sort of interest except the Parnell crisis.

(Lloyd George to Tom Ellis, 27th November 1890, National Library of Wales, Aberystwyth, Ellis Papers).

E.9   I cannot express to you the regret Evans and I felt at your absence during the *Tithe* fight. It was such a glorious struggle for Wales. Wales practically monopolized the attention of the house for fully three weeks. To my mind, that is the great fact of the *Tithe Bill* opposition.

     You may have learned of the new *Disestablishment* Campaign the Welsh National Council proposed initiating. A skeleton scheme has been formulated by the Joint Executive and unless the very regrettable jealousies of the North & South Wales *Federations* upset the business I think it is bound to succeed.

     We young Welshmen are jolly glad to hear that you are on your way back. I fancy we shall have another Welsh fight over free education. Don't you think so? Of course you have heard of our splendid victory of the *Local Veto Bill*. Quite unexpected as the Welshmen were all absent with the exception of 7 staunch teetotallers amongst them.

(Lloyd George to Tom Ellis, 11th April 1891, National Library of Wales, Aberystwyth, Ellis Papers).

E.10   One of the main elements of Mr Lloyd George's character is *push*. He is largely endowed, too, with worldly wisdom. A superficial observer of the man may pronounce him rash and indiscreet; all who are thoroughly familiar with his history will, however, unite in saying that his rashness and indiscretion must be more apparent than real, for they always prove advantageous to him as a party politician by strengthening his position in his constituency and in the country generally. Even this little revolt of his, untimely though it may seem to most of us, will tell hereafter, we feel confident, to his advantage. It is distinctly in his favour that he has the courage to revolt at all. If the Government yield to his demands, great will be his reward; if the Government decline to yield to his demands, great will be the disgrace in the sight of the Welsh people, not of Lloyd George, but of the members who have refused to follow his lead. But why did he revolt? Was it because he felt that he must do something heroic, something sensational, if the attention of his countrymen was to be distracted from his complete discomfiture in the Welsh *Disestablishment* Debate? If the revolt is to be regarded as a tactical movement designed for some such purpose as this, it must be acknowledged to have turned out a perfect success. The courageous little rebel has entirely over-shadowed the fallen parliamentary champion of Welsh *Disestablishment*.

Mr George has a very interesting personality. He is very affable, very frank and outspoken. He has a bright and intelligent face and (in private life) very pleasing manners. One hardly knows what a Campbellite-*Particular Baptist* ought to look like, but one has no difficulty in bringing before one's mental eye the typical outward characteristics of a popular demagogue. These are by no means the outward characteristics of Mr Lloyd George.

He once delivered a powerful speech on Temperance in the House of Commons; he has delivered many equally powerful speeches on the subject in his constituency. He is one of the half-dozen total abstainers in the ranks of the Welsh parliamentary party.

Take him for all in all, he seems by far the best-fitted of the Welsh members for the leadership of the National party in the House of Commons . . . He is quick-witted; he is eloquent; he is daring; in a word, he is perhaps the truest Celt that Wales has ever sent into the House of Commons.

(*T. Marchant Williams*, 'Mr David Lloyd George', in *The Welsh Members of Parliament*, 1894, Cardiff, p.26).

E.11   Dear Mr *Asquith*,
I understand that a deputation of Welsh members propose waiting upon you to press for the adoption by the Govt. of Mr

Lloyd George's amendment to substitute a national council for the Commissioners to be appointed under the Welsh Church Bill. I think that you ought to be acquainted with the fact that the Welsh members are by no means unanimous on the question. I was present at the first meeting of the Welsh members at which the amendment was discussed and strenuously opposed it. The sense of the meeting was so evidently against it that Mr Lloyd George proposed to adjourn the discussion stating that the amendment would not be reached for some time and this was agreed to. I was not present at the next meeting and I think if you will enquire of the deputation you will find that there was only a small minority of the members present and so Mr Lloyd George got his way.

The Church party may support the omission of the word commissioners but they will certainly strenuously oppose the substitution of National Council therefor.

The object is to help on the question of Welsh Home Rule, a movement that has no hold whatever on the Welsh people at large. When it was first mooted in my constituency, I opposed it on the ground that we ought not to fritter away our strength in starting new and crude movements but rather to concentrate on the question of *disestablishment* & nothing more was heard of it in *Eifion*.

I hope the Government will stick to the Bill on this point & if that is done the support of the amendment will collapse.

(J. Bryn Roberts, MP, to H. H. Asquith, 18th May 1895, Bodleian Library, Oxford, Asquith Papers).

E.12   It is not, however, strictly accurate to say that we 'accepted' Ll. George's amendment, and I think you showed rather too great a tendency to whitewash him after the underhand & disloyal fashion in wh. he undoubtedly acted. So far as I remember, he had no associate or apologist among the Welsh members.

(H. H. Asquith to Tom Ellis, 30th November 1895, National Library of Wales, Aberystwyth, Ellis Papers).

E.13   Got a capital meeting last night altho' the audience in these semi-English districts are not comparable to those I get in the

Welsh districts. Here the people have sunk into a morbid footballism.

(Lloyd George to Mrs Lloyd George, 19th November 1895, from Tredegar. National Library of Wales, Aberystwyth).

E.14 The meeting of the *Federation* was a packed one. Associations supposed to be favourable to us were refused representation & men not elected at all received tickets. There were two points of dispute between us. By some oversight they allowed me to speak on one & we carried it – as it turned out not because the majority of the meeting was with us but because they went to the vote immediately after my speech & I can assure you the impression made could be felt. I simply danced upon them. So they refused to allow me to speak on the second point. The majority present were Englishmen from the Newport districts. The next step is that we mean to summon a Conference of South Wales & to fight it out. I am in bellicose form & don't know when I can get home.

(Lloyd George to Mrs Lloyd George, 16th January 1896, from Newport. National Library of Wales, Aberystwyth).

E.15 The meeting was disgracefully packed with Newport Englishmen.

(Lloyd George to Herbert Lewis, 16th January 1896, Penucha MSS, National Library of Wales, Aberystwyth).

E.16 Before this number will have appeared, the first Session of the present Parliament will have closed. Welshmen have reason to be proud of the achievements of their members. It has, in one sense, been the most Welsh session on record. If you look through the 'unfathomable bog' of *Hansard*, you will light upon the name of a Welsh member almost on every page. Mr Lloyd George has more than justified the high opinions that were entertained of him by his friends. Some cavillers used to think – or, at least, to say – that Mr George was only effective when he appealed to the prejudices of the most ignorant among his countrymen. 'He carries no influence except among the mob'

we were told. 'If you want a man of weight you must go to Mr
Solemn Heavyside or Mr Pompous Verbosity.' We were even
told to distrust Mr George's undoubted eloquence. 'Of course',
said they, 'Lloyd George is a good speaker – of a sort. He can
rouse the enthusiasm of a crowd; he can talk most eloquently of
Nationalism and *Cymru Fydd* and such vague things; but he is
not a statesman or a debater. He is excellent on a popular
platform – but he is a nobody in the House. There it is men like
Mr Sprightly Keen and Mr Fluent Commonplace who are
listened to with attention and respect.' Of course these critics
knew all about it – for did they not spend a night in the House of
Commons two years ago, and, if I remember rightly, was it not
Mr Lloyd George himself who procured admission for them?

This session, if it has done nothing else, has, at all events, put
a stop to this idle chatter. Mr George is recognised to-day as the
finest Parliamentarian that Wales has yet sent to the House of
Commons, for with infinitely little resources he has 'scored'
repeatedly over the 'strongest Government of modern times'.
Sir William Harcourt paid the young member for Caernarvon a
handsome compliment publicly on the floor of the House for
the way in which he has fought the *Tory* Government; but
even stronger expressions of admiration have been used by
politicians on both sides of the House in private. Mr Lloyd
George not only has shown an intimate knowledge of the rules
of the House, a readiness in debate, and a keen perception of the
weak points of the *Tory* case, but he has been able, by this pluck
and resolution, to do more than any other man to infuse a new
courage into the Liberal ranks, and to discredit the methods and
the policy of an overbearing majority. For all that, I humbly
think that Mr George did greater work last year than this. This
year he has only been called upon to show 'grit' and cleverness
in fighting the enemy; last year he was put to a far more severe
test – of standing up for principle against his friends.

(W. Llewellyn Williams, 'Through Welsh Spectacles', *Young
Wales*, August 1896, p.192).

E.17   I spoke in the House today *a chefais hwyl anarferol*. Glad I did it.
Was a bit ashamed of my silence but I could not break the ice for

the first time. You have no idea what a feeling it is. I pitched into them as they had not been pitched into before. Hit straight from the shoulder. Wish you had been there. I got my chance & used it. The Government had published a false translation of the *Transvaal* documents! Just think of that. I bullied the Speaker almost. Joe [Joseph Chamberlain (1836–1914): Colonial Secretary] got him to call me to order for saying it was done deliberately. I retorted that if it was not done deliberately then the negligence was a criminal one seeing that it had sent hundreds of brave men already to their death. Either criminal negligence or forgery. I leave it to the right honourable gentleman to elect. It doesn't matter to me which. The Radicals cheered. Of course I said *Chamberlain* personally could not have been guilty of such a thing. But I said someone has & I want to know who. I have never uttered such home truths in that House & no one replied to me. They seemed quite flabbergasted for the moment.

(Lloyd George to Mrs Lloyd George, 27th October 1899, National Library of Wales, Aberystwyth).

E.18   Whatever differences there may exist as to the South African War, no one disputes that Mr Lloyd-George has gained great political distinction during the last two years. Hitherto, his fame was mostly confined within the borders of Wales; and, perhaps, some future historian will say that Wales blundered in not asserting a monopoly over Mr George's talents such as Ireland has always asserted over her most brilliant sons. But Wales' loss has been England's gain, and at a time of great political dearth in political leadership, it has been no small help to English Radicals that they should receive such a timely reinforcement.

    When Mr Lloyd George emerged from boyhood, his uncle was ambitious that he should enter some profession. The law presented itself as the easiest, and, with the help of his uncle, Mr Lloyd-George was able to serve his articles. He and his brother passed through the necessary training, and settled down in *Criccieth* as professional solicitors in a small way of business. It was the time of *Tory* supremacy. The political representation of Wales had long been in the hands of the Conservatives, with the exception of a few weak-kneed, elderly *Whigs*. But Young Wales was on the warpath, and, already, that movement had begun which has regenerated the Welsh Party, and given the succession to youth and enterprise. The question most to the front in the latter eighties throughout North Wales was that of the *tithes*. The attempts of the Church to assert their claims to the utmost had awakened a spirit of bitter resentment among the people. This frequently took the form of forcible resistance to the claims of the *tithe*-owners. The result was that the owners appealed to the law, and many of the farmers and peasants were brought into court. Mr Lloyd George took up their cases, and it was in the zealous and successful defence of the farmers and peasants of Carnarvonshire that he first earned his reputation as a speaker. It was in the Carnarvonshire Courts that he first displayed those qualities of dash and energy which have since made him famous. His legal reputation quickly spread through Carnarvonshire, and a happy chance enabled the Liberals of the day to adopt him as their champion. In 1890, a by-election occurred at the Carnarvon Boroughs, which had hitherto been held securely by the Conservatives. Several names were brought forward in the Liberal Association for the candidature, and among them was that of young Lloyd-George. He was but 26 years of age, and it was natural that the older men should raise many objections to the nomination of a mere youth for an important Welsh constituency. Until quite recently, he had scarcely been heard of, and it seemed a very rash thing to take him on such slender credentials. But it was always the good fortune of Mr Lloyd-George that his own friends have believed in him more than his acquaintances. They all supported him on this occasion, and proved sufficiently in earnest to carry the point. The Tories put up a powerful candidate to oppose him in the chief local landlord, Mr Hugh Ellis-Nanney, and, for a few weeks, the eyes of the country were centred upon the fight. The issue hung in the balance, and it seemed scarcely possible that Mr Lloyd-George should succeed. Finally, he gained the seat by a bare majority, and thus went into the House of Commons at an age when many men have scarcely emerged from a university.

His record since 1890 is probably in the minds of all my readers, and a few words will suffice to sum it up here. Its main feature has undoubtedly been his manful championship of the cause of Welsh nationality – his attack on the Welsh Church, his defence at all times of Welsh Nonconformists, his zeal for unsectarian education, his passionate love for his own people.

He has fought election after election in the Carnarvonshire Boroughs, gradually increasing his majority in the face of most hostile forces. Often have his foes prophesied defeat, but always in vain. His chief opponent has retired into private life, with a consolatory knighthood. Sir John Puleston, a powerful *Tory* knight, came, saw, and was conquered. Now, ambitious young Tories shirk the task of assailing the Carnarvon Boroughs. Across the water from *Criccieth* you can see the hills of Merionethshire, which invite Mr Lloyd-George to a safe seat and easy repose. But that would be to repeat the blunder of Antaeus. Wisely he remains on his own ground, and knows that every effort spent on his native soil adds to his strength at Westminster. From each election he goes back to Parliament stronger; and never stronger than at the Election of 1900, when, in spite of all sinister hopes, he went back with a doubled majority.

For a young man of 37, this is surely a remarkable career. Here is a man without university training, without high birth, without riches, who has already climbed to a high political reputation. What is the secret of his power? I answer – Character. Mr Lloyd George has now plenty of self-acquired culture. He has read many books, and he has travelled much during the last ten years. But all these things are but the trappings – the garnishings of the real man. His root-power lies far beyond anything that is received by training or education. It lies in a certain fund of unexhausted strength, a certain fount of aboriginal power. He is not yet 'sickled o'er with the pale cast of thought'. Take a recent event in his career – the purchase of the *Daily News*. While all the wise men of the Liberal Party were shrugging shoulders and drawing long faces, when experience and prudence were being recruited to swell the forces of despair, when all the warriors were gazing hopelessly at the apparently impregnable fortresses of Fleet Street, the young shepherd went apart, and took his two smooth stones from the brook. It is thus that the giants are killed and the heights conquered – by not believing them to be unconquerable. Thus, action has its root in faith, and hoary wisdom is ashamed. It is said that when a friend protested to *Mirabeau* that a thing was impossible, he replied angrily, – 'Do not utter that foolish word in my presence'. In that, at any rate Mr Lloyd George is like *Mirabeau*. He has cut out the word 'impossible' from his vocabulary.

But the audacity of *Mirabeau* was the audacity of contempt and pride. It was beaten by the facts. The audacity of Lloyd George has a deeper root. He believes in the goodness of men. He believes that in the worst pass you can always rally the good in man if you call it out in the right way. He can remove mountains because he believes in humanity.

(Harold Spender, 'Mr D. Lloyd George MP', in *Young Wales*, March 1901, pp.67–9).

E.19   Ll. G. showed tremendous determination & driving force in carrying the thing through. It remains to be seen whether it will lead to the educational unification of Wales or not . . .

Lloyd George came to the second meeting, swept everything before him in the most peremptory fashion, & carried them in favour of the English plan. I had a chat with him at his office this morning & learnt that his plan was to preserve uniformity throughout Wales in order that we might ultimately have a *Central Board for Wales* for elementary as well as intermediate purposes.

(J. Herbert Lewis's diary, 11th November 1902, Penucha MSS).

E.20   The situation in Wales is becoming exceedingly interesting. The leading Church laity are showing a marked disposition to accept the terms which I have induced some of the Welsh County Councils and the whole body of the Welsh Liberal members to offer them. The proceedings at the conference of Welsh County Councils held at Llandrindod on Friday were quite dramatic in their unanimity. Several Tories had come there to fight but after a dialogue between *Lord Kenyon* and myself, in the course of which the general outline of the terms suggested was remarked, all these Conservatives and Churchmen enthusiastically accepted the proposed compromise and undertook to urge their clerical leaders to agree to a conference.

The Welsh *Tory* Press is also veering round. There is today in the *Western Mail* a strong letter from the Vicar of Swansea, who is probably the most popular clergyman in South Wales, strongly advocating the acceptance of my proposals.

(Lloyd George to W. Robertson Nicoll, 3rd March 1903, Nicoll MSS).

E.21 Having had no literary education himself, [Lloyd George] is unable to realize the needs of the education system. He regards it simply as a political scaffolding and so long as he can see his way to set up the scaffolding he does not trouble himself with the character of the edifice.

(A. C. Humphreys-Owen, MP, to Lord Rendel, 18th June 1905, National Library of Wales, Aberystwyth, Rendel Papers).

E.22 Lloyd George has practically nothing to say for Labour . . . Has Lloyd George, the talented son of the people, nothing better to offer than a wrecked *Education Act*, a baffled aristocratic Church party and a pilloried *Chamberlain*. It seems he has not.

(*Labour Leader*, 16th June 1905).

E.23 The agitation about Welsh *Disestablishment* is becoming a little menacing. The Nonconformist Ministers are afraid it is being squeezed out by more urgently pressed claims & they have summoned a great Conference for next Thursday to pass strong resolutions & I have no doubt to make stronger speeches in support of them . . .

There is a good deal to be said for all this anxiety & I think their demand reasonable. Wales has returned Liberal majorities for *Disestablishment* since 1865. *Gladstone* then put them off for 30 years. They are afraid that Wales being small & silent may be forgotten even now.

I wish you could see your way to send me a strong letter. You have no better friends than these half-insurgent Welsh ministers . . .

(Lloyd George to Sir Henry Campbell-Bannerman, 5th October 1907, British Library, Campbell-Bannerman Papers).

E.24   What is and has been our programme? First of all stands the establishment of complete civil and religious equality. Nonconformity is the religion of the working men of Wales, and to demand equal treatment for the Free Churches in every school maintained out of public funds, and equal position for those Churches in the eye of the law in all things is simply to put forward the claim that the religious institutions of the people shall not be regarded as inferior by the State to those patronised by the aristocracy of the land.

   What is our next legislative idea? The emancipation of the Welsh peasant, the Welsh labourer, and the Welsh miner from the oppression of the antiquated and sterilising and humiliating system of land tenure. Who are more concerned in the success of this part of our programme than the workmen of Wales? Both villager and town workman are vitally interested in the settlement of this problem. The present state of things on the land means that the sustenance of the labouring man is often sacrificed to the sport of the idle few; that almost as large a share of the produce of the soil goes into paying for the permission to cultivate it as is allotted towards maintaining the labourers who till it through the sweat of their brow; that the continued enjoyment of the fruits of the labour of the whole of the rural community may depend upon the caprice of one man. Surely this is enough matter of itself to call for reform. But that is not all. The man who flees from this tyranny into the town is preceded by it there into the recesses of its darkest slum.

   What more have we inscribed on our Welsh national programme? There is the calling in of the aid of the State, which means the concentrated power of all, to assist the moral reformer in the creation of a nation of sober people. How? By removing the temptation to inebriety by interposing legal obstacles in the way of excessive drinking; by so improving the conditions and environments of the people that the despair of squalor shall not drive them to drink. Drink has kept the workmen of this country back a whole generation on the road to progress. It is also an essential part of our national programme to bring the best and highest educational facilities within the reach of the poorest child in the land. We have already done more to achieve this object within the last thirty years than any nation in these islands, but we have only just begun. There is nothing more essential to the permanent emancipation of the working classes of this country than that they should be thoroughly trained in the schools of the land for the struggles in front of them. To crown all, we seek the extension of the powers of self-government to Wales so as to enable her sons and daughters to manage her affairs without hindrance or embarrassment from those who possess neither the time nor the inclination to attend to them, or even to acquire any adequate knowledge as to what these affairs are. No candidate can ever hope successfully to contest an industrial constituency in Wales who does not pledge himself unreservedly to advance these reforms to the best of his power and opportunity. I cannot imagine any genuine Labour candidate desiring to do anything else. Therefore I say confidently that the Labour movement contains no menace for Welsh nationalism.

(Lloyd George, speech to Welsh National Liberal Council, Cardiff, 11th October 1906, *South Wales Daily News*, 12 October, 1906).

E.25   British Liberalism is not going to repeat the errors of Continental Liberalism. The fate of Continental Liberalism should warn them of that danger. It has been swept on one side before it had well begun its work, because it refused to adapt itself to new conditions. The Liberalism of the Continent concerned itself exclusively with mending and perfecting the machinery which was to grind corn for the people. It forgot that the people had to live whilst the process was going on, and people saw their lives pass away without anything being accomplished. But British Liberalism has been better advised. It has not abandoned the traditional ambition of the Liberal party to establish freedom and equality; but side by side with this effort it promotes measures for ameliorating the conditions of life for the multitude.

The old Liberals in this country used the natural discontent of the people with the poverty and precariousness of the means of subsistence as a motive power to win for them a better, more influential, and more honourable status in the citizenship of their native land. The new Liberalism, while pursuing this great political ideal with unflinching energy, devotes a part of its endeavour also to the removing of the immediate causes of discontent. It is true that men cannot live by bread alone. It is equally true that a man cannot live without bread. Let Liberalism proceed with its glorious work of building up the temple of liberty in this country, but let it also bear in mind that the worshippers at that shrine have to live.

It is a recognition of that elemental fact that has promoted legislation like the *Old Age Pensions* Act. It is but the beginning of things. Legislation of this character is essentially just, and it is a severe reflection on our civilisation that we should have waited so long ere we undertook the making of a provision of that kind for the aged and deserving poor. There are 43 millions of people in this country. They are not here of their own choice. Whether they are here by accident or the direct decree of Providence, at any rate they had no control or voice in the selection of the land of their birth. If hundreds and thousands of them either starved or were on the brink of starvation, we must not blame Providence for this misfortune. There are abundant material resources in this country to feed, clothe, and shelter them all – yea, and if properly husbanded and managed, to do the same for many millions more.

(Lloyd George, speech to Welsh National Liberal Council, Swansea, 1st October 1908, *South Wales Daily News*, 2 October, 1908).

E.26 The Archbishop of Canterbury Randall Davidson was born & bred a Presbyterian. He is a mercenary soldier & general of the English Establishment.

Lloyd George trusts him. I have never done so, & I have known him for longer than Lloyd George, whose lack of bitterness & human friendliness in controversy are splendid qualifications but sometimes cause him to be over-generous to opponents. When in full cry his bark is most animating & exciting but I think he never bites. At any rate there is never venom, not even gall, . . . The *Tory* & Society denunciations of his platform style are all based on its utter frankness &

simplicity. He is thought rude & vulgar, and held guilty of degrading his great office. No credit is given him for real chivalry and fairness to opponents. Think of Chamberlain or even *Disraeli* & their rancour and bitterness! There is neither snobbishness nor uncharitableness in Lloyd George. And to me his total want of pose or pretension is a charm of character as well as manner that more than compensates for any occasional over-freedom of expression.

(Lord Rendel to Principal T. F. Roberts, Christmas Day, 1909, University College of Wales, Aberystwyth, archives).

E.27   I shall be glad to find myself in the car starting. I am not cut out for Court life. I can see some of them revel in it. I detest it. The whole atmosphere reeks with *Tory*ism. I can breathe it & it depresses & sickens me. Everybody very civil to me as they would be to a dangerous wild animal whom they fear & perhaps just a little admire for its suppleness & strength. The King is hostile to the bone to all who are working to lift the workmen out of the mire. So is the Queen. They talk exactly as the late King & the *Kaiser* talked to me if you remember about the old Railway strike. 'What do they want striking?' 'They are very well paid', etc.

(Lloyd George to Mrs Lloyd George, 16th September 1911, from Balmoral, National Library of Wales, Aberystwyth).

E.28   Ah! The world owes much to the little five-foot-five nations. The greatest art in the world was the work of little nations; the most enduring literature of England came when she was a nation the size of Belgium fighting a great Empire. The heroic deeds that thrill humanity through generations were the deeds of little nations fighting for their freedom. Yes, and the salvation of mankind came through a little nation . . . Wales must continue doing her duty. I should like to see a Welsh Army in the field. I should like to see the race that faced the Normans for hundreds of years in a struggle for freedom, the race that helped to win *Crecy*, the race that fought for a generation under *Glendower* against the greatest captain in Europe – I should like to see that race give a good taste of its quality in this struggle in Europe; and they are going to do it.

(Lloyd George, speech at Queen's Hall, London, 19th September 1914).

E.29   There is a great deal of difference between the temptation to leave your work for the pleasure of being cramped up in a suffocating malodorous chapel listening to some superstitions I had heard thousands of times before & on the other hand the temptation to have a pleasant ride on the river in the fresh air with a terminus at one of the loveliest gardens in Europe. [Mrs Lloyd George had scolded her husband for going for a trip on the river with S. T. Evans, MP, on a Sunday, instead of going to chapel.]

(Lloyd George to Mrs Lloyd George, 13th August 1890, National Library of Wales, Aberystwyth).

E.30   Your joint telegram as to the action taken by the Government in reference to the bombing school incident gave me a great shock, and I immediately wired you my first impressions. I think it an unutterable piece of insolence, but very characteristic of this Government. They crumple up when tackled by Mussolini and Hitler, but they take it out of the smallest country in the realm which they are misgoverning. It is the way cowards try to show that they are strong by bullying. They run away from anyone powerful enough to stand up to them and they take it out of the weak. In the worst days of Irish coersion [sic], trials were never taken out of Ireland into the English courts. They might be removed from Roscommon to Dublin, but they were never taken to the *Old Bailey*. I cannot recall a single instance in the past of its having been done in the case of Wales. Certainly not in a criminal case. This is the first Government that has tried Wales at the *Old Bailey*. I wish I were there, and I certainly wish I were 40 years younger. I should be prepared to risk a protest which would be a defiance. If I were *Saunders Lewis* I would not surrender at the *Old Bailey*; I would insist on their arresting me, and I am not sure that I would not make it difficult for them to do that. This Government will take no heed of protests which do not menace it. I hope the Welsh Members will make a scene, and an effective one, in the House.

(Lloyd George to Megan Lloyd George, 1st December 1936, from Jamaica, National Library of Wales, Aberystwyth).

Debating the Evidence

Kenneth O. Morgan's selection of sources is, inevitably, largely literary since he is concerned to try to unravel some of the complexities of Lloyd George's relationship with his native country. This relationship, as with everything about Lloyd George, was inordinately complex. In essence, we might expect the greatest light to be shed on it by Lloyd George himself – hence extracts from his letters and diary – and those best acquainted with him, personally and politically, hence assessments of him by fellow politicians.

Here again we have examples of a vitally important corpus of historical sources. It should be stressed that literary sources are not confined to what is conventionally meant by literature. Certainly novels and poetry can be valuable historical sources in their way. But we use the term 'literary sources' to cover a much wider range of written materials. The term covers the kind of sources available here – letters, diaries and journal articles which are a personal response to, and judgement of, individuals or events. Such sources pose their own difficulties of interpretation, but are enormously rich in potential. It is one of the sadnesses of the contemporary historian that the ubiquitous telephone has so adversely affected the amount of personal (as opposed to official) correspondence.

Source E.1

From the evidence in the document what would you need to know about the political context before being able to make good use of the excerpt?

Source E.3

This is obviously a very personal letter. What use is material of this kind to the historian?

Source E.5

What reservations might you have about using a political speech as evidence? Distinguish between the witting testimony, or intentional record, in this speech and the unwitting testimony, or unintentional record.

Source E.6

What are the strengths and weaknesses of this source in helping us decide on the attitude of Lloyd George to Welsh problems in 1890?

Source E.7

How far is the evidence in this document consistent with that in documents E.2 and E.3 in helping us towards an assessment of Lloyd George's personality?

Source E.9

What information would you need before you could make good use of this document? Where might you set about finding such information?

Source E.10

What would you need to know about *T. Marchant Williams* before being able to assess the merits of this extract? How far is this assessment compatible with what you know of Lloyd George from the previous document?

Source E.11

On the basis of the evidence in this document would you regard *J. Bryn Roberts* as a useful witness in your assessment of Lloyd George?

Sources E.13 to E.16

How far is the evidence in these documents compatible and how far contradictory? What reasons might there be for both of these features?

Source E.17

Does this document indicate any difficulties in assessing Lloyd George's motives in opposing the *Boer War*?

Source E.18

What further information would you require about Harold Spender and about the journal for which he wrote before making good use of this assessment of Lloyd George?

Sources E.21 and E.22

These documents give information about Lloyd George but what do they tell us of A. C. Humphreys-Owen and the writer in the *Labour Leader*?

Source E.24

Given the context in which this document came into existence how much reliance would you place on the information in it? Distinguish here between intentional and unintentional record.

Sources E.27 and E.28

Are there any paradoxes evident in these two documents taken together? What do they tell us about Lloyd George, if anything?

Sources E.29 and E.30

How far are these documents evidence of the complexity of Lloyd George's relationship with Wales and things Welsh? What information would you require before being able to answer this question?

Discussion

It is important that in this series of essays on Wales 1880–1914 there should be one which deals with a personality. When that personality is as complex as Lloyd George the problems with researching into and writing about personalities are more obvious.

Lloyd George is one of the most complex and paradoxical characters ever to have dominated Welsh and British politics. The enigma of Lloyd George is not due to lack of evidence. The primary evidence we have about him is enormous. He spent most of his life in Parliament and for 17 years held high office. *Hansard* records all his House of Commons speeches. Parliamentary papers record the legislation, some of the most

Lloyd George speaking at Killerton Park, Devon, in 1925. (*Source: BBC Hulton Picture Library*)

significant this century, for which he was responsible. Cabinet records and private office papers record yet more about his career in Government. There is no lack of information as to what he did and what he said. The enigma remains. *Why* did he do what he did in public life? *Why* did he embrace the causes which he did, and forsake them? What blend of idealism, realism and cynicism motivated him?

Few politicians have had their private life dissected to the extent which has been the case with Lloyd George; few have led such interesting private lives. But the paradoxes of the private life bear on those of the public persona, inevitably, and so are a matter of endless fascination. Here again, more surprisingly, we are not short of sources. Lloyd George's diaries and, above all, his letters, record his reactions, feelings and attitudes to public and private matters in some detail. The short selection in the documents section here gives a glimpse of their scope. Yet the paradox remains. Few politicians have left such a corpus of documentation in their wake. Few men of affairs have generated so much in the way of articles, books and biographies. There are obviously no definitive answers to questions about Lloyd George.

In microcosm, the reasons for this are evident in the selection of documents provided by Dr Morgan. They deal with only some of the great range of questions which a study of Lloyd George's career generates, that of his relationship with the people, institutions and ethos of his country of Wales. This matter itself is inordinately complex, as Dr Morgan has shown. Lloyd George probably genuinely loved aspects of Wales, and also exploited his Welshness. He was the object of unadulterated adulation from the mass of Welsh people, yet has often been accused of forsaking the interests of his country for his own self interest. His genius inspired awe and envy; his ruthlessness inspired admiration and hatred; the maverick inspired delight and distrust – the latter especially among the Establishment.

Against this background where do we begin to assess the 'truth' of the documents which Dr Morgan has provided. They are not documents of record, like censuses or court records. As literary documents they provide their own problems of interpretation. Some of the documents are assessments of Lloyd George made by fellow politicians in contemporary journals. First, we need to know whether they were friends or enemies, political associates or opponents or perhaps relatively disinterested commentators. But they remain personal assessments, more or less well-informed, certainly, but still one person's view of another. There is valuable unwitting testimony in them all – for example they show just how much interest Lloyd George generated among his contemporaries, but the witting testimony in them has to be treated extremely cautiously.

When then of the letters and diaries of Lloyd George himself? Surely here we are in touch with the man. Up to a point, perhaps. But what are diaries except daily autobiographies? And we know how politicians' autobiographies are normally exercises in self-justification. And how selective are Lloyd George's letters to his wife – either when dealing with his personal life or his political life? This might seem unduly cynical. Certainly some of the letters here ring true – those dealing with his enormous ambition, for example. Yet all such literary sources need to be considered with the utmost care. Expression of opinion needs to balanced against action at every opportunity. If this were not so, the amount of research which scholars like Dr Kenneth Morgan and scores of others have devoted to Lloyd George would have long since come up with definitive answers. What that research has done is to make the parameters of the argument and discussion more closely defined. But the assessment of this genius of a Welshman by his compatriots and others, remains controversial. It is in the nature of such evidence as we have here that it should be so.

Further Reading

Books

A. Clayre, *Work and Play*, London, 1974.

Don Cregier, *Bounder from Wales*, Missouri, 1976.

Victor E. Durkacz, *The Decline of the Celtic Languages*, Edinburgh, 1983.

Hywel Francis and David Smith, *The Fed: A History of the South Wales Miners in the 20th Century* (esp. Ch.1), London, 1980.

William George, *My Brother and I*, London, 1958.

W. R. P. George, *Lloyd George: Backbencher*, Llandysul, 1983.

W. R. P. George, *The Making of Lloyd George*, London, 1976.

John Grigg, *The Young Lloyd George*, London, 1973.

Bob Holton, *British Syndicalism 1900–1914*, (esp. Ch.5), London, 1976, pbk.

D. Howell, *Land and People in Nineteenth-Century Wales*, London, 1978.

Martin Hoyles, ed., *The Politics of Literacy*, London, 1983.

Stephen Humphries, *Hooligans or Rebels*, Oxford, 1981.

D. Jenkins, *The Agricultural Community in South-West Wales at the turn of the Twentieth Century*, Cardiff, 1971.

R. M. Jones, *The North Wales Quarrymen*, Cardiff, 1981.

R. Tudur Jones, *Ffydd ac Argyfwng Cenedl*, Llandysul, 1981.

P. J. Leng, *The Welsh Dockers*, Ormskirk, 1981.

Kenneth O. Morgan, *Lloyd George*, London, 1974.

Kenneth O. Morgan, ed, *Lloyd George: Family Letters 1885–1936*, Cardiff/Oxford, 1973.

Kenneth O. Morgan, *Rebirth of a Nation: Wales 1880–1980*, Cardiff/Oxford, 1981: pbk., 1982.

Kenneth O. Morgan, *Wales in British Politics 1868–1922*, Cardiff, 3rd edition, 1980.

Richard Price, *An Imperial War and the British Working Class*, London, 1971.

David Smith and Gareth Williams, *Fields of Praise*, Cardiff, 1982.

Articles

Martin Barclay, ' 'Slaves of the Lamp': The Aberdare Miners' Strike, 1910'. *Llafur*, Vol.II, 1980, 24–42.

Deirdre Beddoe, 'Towards a Welsh Women's History'. *Llafur*, Vol.III, 1981, 32–38.

David Egan, 'The Unofficial Reform Committee and *The Miners' Next Step*'. *Llafur*, Vol.I, 1973, 3–14.

Ieuan Gwynedd Jones, 'Language and Community in 19th Century Wales' in *A People and Proletariat*, ed. D. Smith, London, 1980.

David Smith, 'Tonypandy 1910: Definitions of Community'. *Past and Present*, No.87, May 1980, 158–184.

Brinley Thomas, 'The Migration of Labour into the Glamorganshire Coalfield 1861–1911' in *Industrial South Wales 1750–1914*, ed. W. E. Minchinton. London, 1969.

L. J. Williams, 'The Road to Tonypandy'. *Llafur*, Vol.I, 1973, 3–14.

Glossary

Ablett, Noah

Rhondda-born Marxist miners' leader. Inspirational leader of left-wing socialists in Wales.

Abraham, William (Mabon)

Miners' agent. Liberal MP for Rhondda and first president of *South Wales Miners' Federation*. Believed in a policy of co-operation with the owners.

Annealer

A person involved in the process of toughening tinplate by heat.

Arable Farming

Farming of the land (as opposed to *pastoral farming*, i.e. the farming of animals).

Asquith, H. H.

Liberal MP from 1886. Prime Minister 1908–16. Replaced by Lloyd George, causing what was eventually a disastrous split in the Liberal Party.

Attlee, Clement

Labour MP from 1922. Leader of the party 1935–55. Prime Minister in the Labour government 1945–51.

Auger

Carpenter's tool for boring holes in wood.

Bad rockmen

Quarrymen who disposed of non-usable slate.

Baldwin, Stanley

Conservative MP from 1908. Prime Minister 1923–4, 1924–9, 1935–7. Leading figure in the national government 1931–5.

Balfour, Arthur	Conservative MP from 1874. Prime Minister 1902–5. Leader of the opposition 1906–11.
Ballot Act, 1872	Act of Parliament which legislated that parliamentary elections should be by secret ballot thus limiting improper pressures on voters.
Band of Hope	Youth temperance movement.
Bargain System	Agreement between managers and quarrymen on how much slate should be cut and paid for in one month.
Beauforts	Immensely wealthy ancient landowning family based in Raglan.
Behinder	A skilled job in the tinplate industry.
Blacklegs	Workers who continue to do their jobs during a strike, or who are brought in to do the jobs of those on strike.
Board of Education	Founded in 1899 as the central government agency for administering education.
Boer Wars	The first, 1880–1, occurred when the Boers or Dutch settlers of the Transvaal rebelled against British annexation. The second, 1899–1902, normally called the Boer War, broke out when the Boers invaded Nataal. British forces eventually won, annexing the Orange Free State and the Transvaal.
Brecknock Beacons	Brecon Beacons – the range of hills around Brecon.
Burn	A stream or river.
Bushel	A measure of capacity of eight gallons.
Bute Family of Cardiff	Nineteenth/twentieth-century dynasty of landowners/industrialists – built Cardiff docks and Cardiff Castle.

Butty system	By this system jobs in a coal mine were sub-contracted by the colliery under-manager to the butty who was then responsible for employing the men.
Campbell-Bannerman, Henry	Liberal MP from 1868. Prime Minister 1905–8. Gave self-government to the colonies in South Africa.
Central Welsh Board	Representative body of the Welsh local authorities to inspect and examine intermediate secondary schools in Wales.
Chamberlain, Joseph	Radical Liberal MP from 1876. Led the Liberal Unionist alliance with the Conservatives in opposition to *Irish Home Rule*. Colonial Secretary 1895–1903 at the time of the *Boer War*.
Chancellor	– of the Exchequer.
Chefais hwyl anarferol	'I had unusual inspiration'.
Churchill, Winston	Home Secretary 1910–11. Holder of major government offices at intervals 1908–29. Prime Minister 1940–5, 1951–5.
Clod	Lumps of coal and earth stuck together.
Coal trimmer	A skilled job in the coalmining industry.
Coursing Match	Relates to the 'sport' of hare coursing.
Crecy	1346 battle between Edward III and Philip VI of France. An English victory.
Criccieth	Town in north Wales, home of Lloyd George.
Cutting bottom	Cleaning an area of the floor in preparation for getting at the coal seam.
Cymanfa Ganu	Singing festival.
Cymru and *Cymru'r Plant*	Magazines in Welsh for adults and children founded and edited by O. M. Edwards.

Cymru Fydd	Started 1892. Supporters Tom Ellis, Lloyd George and D. A. Thomas. A Welsh national movement for Welsh independence.
Daniel, D. R.	Secretary of the North Wales Quarrymen's Union 1896. Great friend of *Tom Ellis* and O. M. *Edwards.*
Davitt, Michael	One of the leaders of the movement for Irish independence in the nineteenth century. Organizer of the Irish Land League.
Demography	Study of population sizes.
Diaconate	Board of Deacons or elected 'middle management' of nonconformist chapels.
Disestablishment	— withdrawal of state control from a church — in this instance the Church in Wales withdrawing from the state Church of England.
Disraeli, Benjamin	Conservative MP from 1837. Prime Minister 1868 and 1874–80.
Dissent	Nonconformist denominations which had broken away from the established church.
Education Act 1902	Act of Parliament which made Local Education Authorities of the county and county borough councils and the urban district councils the local controlling bodies for education.
Edwards, Sir Owen M.	Historian, literatteur, academic. Chief Inspector of the Welsh Department of the Board of Education, 1907–20.
Eifion	Eifionydd – a district of the Llŷn peninsula in north-west Wales.
Elders	Elected 'middle management' in certain nonconformist denominations especially the Presbyterians.

Elias, John	Famous Calvinistic Methodist preacher. Died 1841. Ministered in north Wales.
Ellis, Tom	Son of tenant farmer. Liberal MP for Merioneth from 1886. Liberal Chief Whip 1894. Highly talented Welsh leader. Particularly associated with *Cymru Fydd*.
Evans, Christmas	One of the most famous of Welsh preachers. Died 1838. Baptist. Native of Cardiganshire. Ministered in north and south Wales. Known for his vivid, imaginative sermons.
Evans, Herber	Draper's assistant who became one of the great Welsh pulpit orators.
Farrier	A person who shoes horses.
Fed, The	The South Wales Miners' Federation founded after the coal dispute of 1898.
Federation	An association of Liberals. In the late nineteenth century north and south Wales were grouped in separate Liberal federations.
Free Church Council	The free churches were the nonconformist denominations.
G.O.M.	– Grand Old Man. *W. E. Gladstone*'s nickname.
Gee, Thomas	Denbigh-born President of the Welsh Land League. Preacher and publisher.
Gladstone, W. E.	MP from 1832. Leader of the Liberal Party from 1867. Four times Prime Minister.
Glendower	Anglicized form of the name Owain Glyndŵr, whose rising against the English king after 1400 gave Wales a brief period of independence.
Gob	An empty space from which coal has been taken in the long-wall system of mining, or the rubbish used to fill it.

Hansard	The official publication which records all the proceedings of Parliament.
Harcourt, Sir William	Liberal MP 1868–98. Home Secretary and Chancellor of the Exchequer. Liberal leader 1896–8.
Hardie, Keir	Coalminer who founded the Scottish Labour Party. First Labour MP – for Merthyr 1892–5, 1900–15.
Horner, Arthur	One of the greatest twentieth-century miners' leaders, involved in the International Brigade in the Spanish Civil War.
Humphreys Owen, A. C.	Liberal MP for Montgomery. Barrister. First Chairman of the *Central Welsh Board*.
Independent Labour Party	Founded 1893. Wanted eight-hour day and collective ownership of the means of production, distribution and exchange in the national economy.
Independents	Welsh-language nonconformist denomination – English language equivalent were Congregationalists.
Irish Home Rule	The movement to give Ireland independence from the rest of Britain.
Kaiser	Emperor of Germany before and during the First World War.
Kenyon, Lord	MP for Denbigh boroughs. Closely involved in the passing of the Welsh Intermediate Education Act 1889.
Keynes, J. M.	Highly influential economist, advocated government intervention to reduce unemployment in the 1930s.
Khaki Election	The election fought after the *Boer War*.

Lewis, Elfed	Nineteenth- and twentieth-century Welsh hymn writer, minister, poet. One of the greatest names in Welsh nonconformity. Born Carmarthenshire.
Lewis, Saunders	One of Wales's greatest Welsh-language playwrights and an influential nationalist. Formulated the philosophy upon which the present-day *Welsh Language Society* is based.
Lewis, Sir J. Herbert	Flintshire-born. Close friend of Lloyd George. MP. Educationalist.
Lloyd George, Megan	Daughter of Lloyd George. Liberal MP, later Labour MP, for Carmarthenshire.
Llŷn	The peninsular part of north-west Wales.
Local Government Act, 1888	Provided for elected county and county borough councils.
Log Books	A daily record of the activities and events, in this case, of school life.
Mabon's Day	A monthly holiday negotiated for miners by *William Abraham (Mabon)* by which the miners were given the first Monday of every month off. Lasted from 1892–8. Stopped by the owners after the 1898 dispute.
McKinley Tariff	Import duties imposed by the United States of America on tinplate.
Metropolitan Police	Police force of London: responsible to the Home Secretary.
MFGB	Miners' Federation of Great Britain. The union of British miners to which the *South Wales Miners' Federation* affiliated in 1899.
Millinery shop	Hat shop.
Mirabeau	French orator and revolutionary. President of the Jacobin club in 1790.

Mond, Sir Alfred	Opened the largest nickel works in the world in Clydach, West Glamorgan in 1902. Liberal MP and eccentric. Staunch supporter of Lloyd George.
Monoglots	Speakers of one language.
Morgans of Tredegar	Owned vastly wealthy estate and industrial resources – lived in Tredegar Park.
Mormons	Members of the Church of Jesus Christ of the Latter Day Saints. Founded in 1830 by Joseph Smith in Salt Lake City, USA.
National Health Insurance	Introduced by the Liberal government to be paid for out of increased taxes in the budget of 1909.
Net loss	Excess of out-migration (emigration) over inward migration (immigration).
New Zealand All Blacks	The New Zealand international rugby team. They play in an all black strip.
North Wales Quarrymen's Union	Set up in 1874. Led to confrontation with the owners.
Old Age Pension	A 1908 scheme introduced by Lloyd George for non-contributory old age pensions.
Old Bailey	The Central Criminal Court in London.
Particular Baptists	Branch of the Baptist denomination.
Pastoral Farming	Farming of animals.
Patagonia	Part of Argentina, settled by Welsh immigrants in the nineteenth century.
Payments in kind	Payments, usually of rent, in goods or services.
Penrhyn, Lord	Head of landowning family in Gwynedd – owned Penrhyn, the largest slate quarry in the world in the early twentieth century.

People's Budget	The budget of 1909. Lloyd George imposed death duties and increased taxes to pay for National Health Insurance and pensions. Provoked a constitutional crisis.
Philadelphia	Major city in Pennsylvania, eastern United States of America.
Piece work	Work done or paid for by the piece or amount produced.
Pleb's League	Group founded by *Ablett* in 1909 believing in class war and the overthrow of capitalism.
Ponc	Gallery in slate quarry.
Rendel, Stuart	Liberal MP for Montgomeryshire. Leader of the Welsh MPs. Friend of Gladstone. Closely involved in the Welsh Intermediate Education Act and Disestablishment.
Rendelism	Pertaining to the policies of *Stuart Rendel*.
Rhys, Morgan John	Radical, author. Founded Welsh settlement in the United States of America.
Roberts, Evan	Led the 1904/5 religious revival in Wales.
Roberts, John Bryn	Died 1931. Solicitor and county court judge. Liberal, opposed Lloyd George's coalition government.
Roberts, Samuel (Snr.)	Independent minister, author. Unsuccessfully tried to found Welsh colony in Tennessee.
Rollerman	A skilled job in the tinplate industry.
Rood	Measure of land.
Roofing	Ripping the top or roof away and making the roof safe before mining coal.
Rubbish men	Quarrymen who piled up the non-usable slate.
Rybelwyr	*Rubbish men.*
Salt Lake City	Headquarters of the *Mormons*.

Singling roots	Taking out excess plants to allow one to grow fully.
Slate dressing	Cutting slate to suitable sizes – mainly for roofing purposes.
Slate splitting	The process of separating slate rock into thin sheets.
Sliding scale	Way of determining miners' wages according to the price of coal.
SWMF	South Wales Miners' Federation. Affiliated to the *Miners' Federation of Great Britain* in 1899.
Sprag	The prop used to support the roof when working a seam of coal.
Stall	The pillar and stall method of mining involved taking coal from an area, leaving a pillar of coal to support the roof. The mined area was the chamber or stall assigned to one miner to work.
Stipendiary Magistrate	Paid magistrate as opposed to voluntary, unpaid justices of the peace.
Thomas, D. A.	Later Lord Rhondda. Liberal MP, coalowner, ally of Lloyd George. Helped create *Cymru Fydd* – and destroy it.
Tithe	The tenth of a person's income given to supporting a church – in this case the established Church of England.
Tithe Act 1891	Act of Parliament by which tithes were subsumed into rent.
Tithe War	Opposition by Nonconformist north Wales' farmers to paying a portion of their income to the Anglican church, sometimes erupting into violence when goods were confiscated for non-payment.
Tory	A twentieth-century alternative name for the Conservative party.

Transvaal	State of South Africa. See *Boer War*.
Treaty of Versailles	The treaty between the allies and Germany after the First World War.
WEA	Workers' Educational Association – provides classes in a wide variety of subjects for adult workers.
Welsh Department of the Board of Education	Founded 1907. Gave Wales some control over the inspection and administration of schools.
Welsh Intermediate Education Act 1889	Act of Parliament which resulted in the founding of a system of secondary education in Wales and consolidated the university college provision.
Welsh Not	Piece of wood put around the necks of pupils who spoke Welsh in schools.
Welsh Language Society	Founded by Beriah Gwynfe Evans in the nineteenth century to foster the Welsh language generally.
Whigs	Nineteenth-century radicals, became the Liberal party later in the nineteenth-century.
Williams, Sir T. Marchant	Died 1914. Barrister and writer. Born Aberdare. Coalminer's son. Schoolmaster, stipendiary magistrate.
Williams, W. Llewellyn	Son of tenant farmer from Llansadwrn. Liberal MP, lawyer, historian, supporter of *Cymru Fydd*.
Y Faner	Nineteenth-century Liberal radical Welsh-language newspaper.

Index